SOMEDAY IS TODAY

Your Journey to living a life filled with passion
and purpose starts TODAY!

James Daniel Andersen

I wish to thank all the people that were involved in writing this. It seems almost impossible to reach everyone, as I believe I am made up of at least a small piece of everyone I have ever met in my life, and many more I haven't. There are some people that contributed larger than others and they probably have a little bigger piece in shaping my experiences. But if I have ever met you, even in a random moment, or through the divine connection that brought my life, its experiences and messages to me, you are more than likely in some way, form or fashion, part of my being and thus part of this book.

I especially want to thank my family and friends for their sometimes vocal and often times silent love, patience and encouragement throughout the many years of listening to me say someday I'm going to write a book.

My wife Maria and children Ashtyn, Owen, Evalynn, Brody and Jovie in particular need a moment of praise. They are my earthly motivation and they have brought me more love, lessons and growth than they will ever know!

PLEASE SHARE YOUR JOURNEY AS JAMES WOULD LOVE TO SHARE HIS

TO CONTACT AUTHOR/SPEAKER FOR AVAILABILITY PLEASE

Send E-mail to:

Jamesandersen33@gmail.com

TABLE OF CONTENTS

FROM THE AUTHOR

IT'S TIME TO DISCOVER YOUR TRUE SELF AND UNCOVER YOUR PASSION AND PURPOSE

Are you looking to attain true inner happiness and peace? Are you searching for purpose? Are you struggling to find your passions and live the way you've always dreamed?

Then this book is for you and the day you decide to start the journey can be today!

I don't know exactly what path you need to take to find what you are looking for. I don't think anyone can answer these questions for you. No one can truly determine what path will lead to the life you have always been meant to live. Only you can discover this for yourself, if you're willing to be honest and stay committed to the quest. Sometimes we have to find out who we are not before we can discover who we are. This book hopes to guide you to a point where you start to see that all personal growth, purpose and fulfillment come from within. And the adventure is as unique and essential to as you are. We all have a particular purpose in this world. You hold the key that unlocks the door to your true self, no one else does, except maybe God, but you still have to work with Him.

You will not find true purpose and fulfillment "out there". You don't have to travel to India and meditate with a spiritual guru, live on a ship with the merchant marines, build wells in Africa or become a missionary to find your purpose or the true meaning of life. Your journey may lead you to these places. But from my experience, if we cannot make an impact in quality of the lives we encounter each and every day in our own homes, communities and places we visit then how do we think we are going to make a difference in places around the world?

This book is a story of some of my experiences, stories, reflections and methods that have been a part of my journey. The simple methods and changes in mindset have helped bring me as close as I possibly can be to my purpose at this time in my life. This book is a culmination of practices and perspectives that have guided me as I explored who I was, who I am and how my inner purpose was always inside me I just needed to uncover it. This book is about taking this process seriously but not taking ourselves so serious and learning to enjoy the journey life throws at us. This book is practical but won't tell you all the answers. What it will do is help you ignite, relate and think about ways that may help you uncover your true self and your passion and purpose.

So just to clarify who this book is for?

This book is for the majority of us who can't necessarily drop everything at this moment and travel abroad or take a month off and experience people and other cultures. This book is for those that would like to live in peace and act with love as they navigate the magic, misery and mystery of everyday life. This book is for those who want to find beauty each and every day, regardless of where they are, what they are doing, who they are with or what life gives them. This book is for those whose circumstances seem irreversible or impossible to overcome. This book is for those who have strived to live the American dream. Only to find out that in the process of wanting more or something grander their own profound dreams they had deep within themselves have been commandeered. This book is for those that want to discover that hiding from or escaping reality doesn't bring you happiness. This book is for those that want to be inspired and in awe of the present moment. This book is for those that have tried it their way only to find out their way isn't working any longer, or maybe it never really did. This book is for those who want to see the world differently and experience the life that they have always dreamed was possible. This book is for those who want to enjoy the gift of life they have, now, not someday.

This book is for YOU!

All I have are my experiences and all you have are yours. All we can do is share our journeys and stories and help each other find our true selves, discover our passions and ultimately share our purpose with the world.

START WHERE YOU
ARE AT RIGHT NOW

We can't start in the past or the future. We can't start where we wish we were or where we want to be. All we can do is start where we are at right now. As you read through this book do me a favor and be present. You can start to build the life you always wanted. But you need to start where you are at right now. We need to learn how to enjoy life in the moment. If we can't seem to find a way out of the mud we are stuck in how do we move forward?

The answer is one moment at a time. We need to appreciate where we are at and realize we have a choice to move in the direction of our purpose each and every day. We need to get away from this mentality of, "I'll be happy when I get more of this or when I accomplish that".

There will be much to contemplate as we endeavor on this journey together throughout this book. My hope is the messages and themes within this book provoke some deep and soulful searching, but most importantly, provoke ACTION! I encourage you to reflect, reread and then act. Reflecting is encouraged but do not fall into morbid reflection. If you find yourself thinking about something that causes you pain or anguish use it as motivation and do something about it. Feel what you feel and let it flow through you and then proceed to read on or take action. Do what is necessary in that moment. Whatever you choose to do about that feeling is up to you. There is no right or wrong there just is.

Seems simple, right?

It may be simple but it's not always easy!

I heard it from a very young age. "Slow down and take a breath". When I got frustrated over something miniscule, my parents would say, "slow down, take a breath". I hope you take a few moments after reading the next page to slow down and breathe. This simple message has done wonders for me. My hope for you is you realize that in your hands is a book with simple messages that have the ability to make a huge difference in your life. The more present you can be while reading this book and practicing some of the methods found within it the more benefit you will gain and the more enduring passion you will have to fulfill your purpose.

But how do we become present?

Becoming present in the moment can be as simple as breathing. One of the best practices to become present in the moment is something that we do every day without typically thinking too much about it. From the moment we arrived out of our mother's womb and took our first breath we were attached to the beauty and mystery of breath.

One of the best ways to gain clarity and discover presence is learning how to breathe. Just be quiet and still with your breath. Our breath is with us in the beginning and will be with us until the end of our physical lives. But many of us will spend our whole lives never learning how or understanding the great power behind being present with our breath.

When I started to learn how to meditate I found out the core of the practice started with the breath. Learning to breathe is the first thing you learn when you enter school to become a Monk. No matter how old you are when you enter Monk school, whether it's five or twenty-five, the first thing you learn how to do is breathe.

There are amazing lifelong advantages of getting in touch with our breath. Focusing on this seemingly simple practice of learning how to breathe will have a profound impact in your life.

When I wake up in the morning, the first thing I do is take a big breath. I thank God and choose to be grateful for the magic of being able to breathe and be blessed with another day to live. I also pray and ask for God to direct my intentions. Otherwise, each and every day I can get pulled in various directions. Without God directing my thoughts and actions I can easily get off course. If I don't have a higher power directing the intent and purpose for my life, then I know my best intentions will fall short.

We make the choice to submerge ourselves in a fast paced society, seeing how much we can pack in our day, but there is hope. There are simple and effective ways to slow down and you can start by learning to breathe throughout your day. With all the running around, deadlines and appointments we need to purposefully schedule time to get ourselves centered. If we practice taking even thirty seconds to breathe deeply and become present it can have a great impact on our well-being. Calm, conscious, slow breathes...feeling the air as it fills your lungs and the flow of warm breath through your nostrils, feeling the sensations as your chest rises and falls, just taking a moment for yourself.

When you get in your car, before rushing off to work, take a moment to relax and breathe. Just take thirty seconds. It connects you with the moment. Neurological science backs up the positive effects of deep conscious breathing and mindfulness. I started practicing becoming conscious to the present moment during these fractions of my day and it has made a big difference in my level of self awareness. Every time we reset and practice this simple method we become more aware and it becomes easier. It naturally forms healthy habit.

Try it! Take in some deep slow breathes to gather your

thoughts. This will help you converse on a much higher train of thought. It will grow your relationships because you will be looking at the solutions and not get caught up in the problems and the emotions of conversations. Before you go into a meeting, or while at your desk before making an uncomfortable phone call, take a moment for yourself to be present and breathe. This thirty second trick will add depth and value to your daily interactions and also reduce stress. Before talking to your children or spouse, co-worker or sibling take a few moments to be still and become aware of how you feel and how precious and miraculous the world is all around you. Everything is connected to the oneness of life.

CHAPTER 1

THE POWER OF PASSION AND PURPOSE

You are a miracle.

You are a miracle. You being created and here to read this is a miracle in itself. Everything that needed to happen and take place precisely at the right time and in the correct order is beyond miraculous. Out of the almost 8 billion people currently on this earth you are the only you. You were born with special traits and gifts uniquely and divinely inspired particularly for you.

When we are formed it is a miracle. At that moment we were instilled to carry within us a miraculous source which forever connects us to the universe.

For children, every day is a new experience, full of miracles and wonderment. But as we grow, somewhere along the way life has a way of turning on us, or more accurately, we turn on it. Life is full of radical and ridiculous twists and turns, each raw, natural, abstract and obscure. Every experience shapes our interpretation of the world and what it means to us.

Life works for us. But when life throws challenges our way sometimes we trade in our gifts, dreams and passions for comfort and ease. These subconscious trades are easier but take us, little by little, farther away from whom we are verses who we are truly meant to be. These trades seem much easier and so minor that we think they don't affect us. They seem much simpler than facing the reality of what we feel. We are inundated to believe it's acceptable and normal as we gradually get lost in the complex world of stimuli pulling us in various directions. Trading what's right for us for the easy way out is a typical response and may seem like the simplest tactic to dull the pain. Oftentimes it does work, temporarily, but it's only a short term solution.

In the long run when we trade in our passions, purpose and dreams for something less than or different than what we were designed and put on earth to do we struggle to find fulfillment.

The only way to be fulfilled in life is to recognize the miracle we are, become aware that life is a gift, grow into our true selves and live out the purpose we were destined to achieve. This is the only way, at this time, I've found to feel truly fulfilled.

It doesn't matter where you are at in life and what you are doing or feeling. The moment we realize we can choose to look at our challenges as growth opportunities, everything we thought we knew about life changes. The change in perception that starts to take place in our mind transforms us. It is but a small seed being planted that we much then nurture. Remember, you cannot pull on a plant to make it grow faster. The challenges, struggles and pains all of a sudden become valuable building blocks for growth.

A lot of us feel like we are just getting through life, well it is time to change that mentality. We are in an age of choice. We can start today to view things we used to perceive as negative or as obstacles, which used to get in the way of our goals and dreams, into new revelations in the journey of expanding our passion, purpose and dreams.

"The secret of getting ahead is getting started" – Mark Twain

You can start today, right now, in this moment; it's simple, if you make a decision to look at yourself and at the world differently. Put down you're old foggy, social norm set of lenses, and put on your new childlike abandoned set of lenses you had when you were a kid. Start today, practicing a new way of thinking, which is really just your natural way of thinking, before you were blinded by your current perception of the world. It's when we start to look at the very beginning of our life that we start to see who we were meant to be. We have a tendency to forget that we have the source of our purpose inside us. Just like the might oak tree or life giving apple tree, we are finely tuned to grow into exactly who we were meant to be.

Sometimes I think how different my life would be if I could start over in first grade knowing what I know now. First grade is one of the simplest times in our lives but also one of the scariest. The reality is I can't start over nor would I want to because I wouldn't be who am I today if I did. If fact, knowing too much before your ready might have a reverse effect on your journey.

It's time to own your journey. Take a moment to reflect on who you were and what made you feel alive before other people, teachers, friends and media explained, told and showed you who you were supposed to be and how you are supposed to feel. What truly makes you feel alive? We may have allowed ourselves over the years to be molded by our demand to be accepted by people and society, but it's never too late, you can start over, right now. Use this moment to honestly appreciate the unique and miraculous person you are...start today by uncovering the layers to find your true self.

Slowly peel the layers off, take your time, this is not an overnight journey. Don't rush as you may miss something that will be useful in the long run. Thoughtful consideration of this process, although uncomfortable at times, will make all the difference. As you start to uncover your true self, a layer at a time, your journey will begin to unfold. You will discover experiences, which have laid dormant, waiting to help guide you rediscover who you are. Those parts of the real you that have been patiently waiting for your recognition again will start to get excited and beg you to keep going.

Today is the Day! It's time to start the greatest adventure of your life. Now light the torch, step into and illuminate the chamber which will unveil the layers which make you who you are! Some nooks of the chamber will be scary and some joyful. But with each layer you will discover your fire for something greater. If you look at it from the right perspective the passion will build and shine an even greater clarity into your inner being and your true self.

Take a moment, set time aside every day and be honest with yourself, realizing who you really are, what makes you unique. Pick a time that works best for you in an environment that makes your mind still. I like doing this in the morning, but sometimes it's over my lunch period or at night. It eventually became something I can do pretty much anytime I have five minutes to spare. More on that later. If you're honest you may like some of the traits you have and there may be other parts of you and thoughts that make your stomach turn a little. It's perfectly ok and normal to be exactly where and who you are right now. If you're ready to change even a little that is progress, and life is all about progress not perfection. We have a tendency to look at the "bad" parts of us. That is just part of who we are right now. It's our ability to look at every part of us and realize the awesomely unique traits, gifts and passions we do have. Don't label them as good or bad, everyone has varying levels. The real testament is if we are willing to proceed in choosing to work towards a better way of living that brings us closer to our true self. The parts of us that we see as negative will provide us with a unique means of relating and helping others.

Make a list of everything about you that makes you, you. Take some time and think back to your earliest memories of what you loved to do and what you dreamed of becoming. No matter how silly, crazy or ridiculous your ideas were or are just remind yourself of what they meant to you. What made you feel filled with that unique happiness you crave once again? Write down what you believe are character traits that are positive and character traits that you interpret at this point as negative. Don't get overwhelmed, this will be a life long journey and some items you may not be ready to write down or work on, yet. Just be honest, that is all that is needed at this point. If you are honest then you are already over half way towards finding your passion and purpose. As you compile your list you will start to see yourself for who you are instead of how you've defined yourself using the world's definition.

With your new set of lenses, with any diligence, you will start to connect to your true self as you currently are and give you a base for who you want to be. As you take this journey backwards into the experiences that shaped your current self, you will set the framework to start shaping a truer path forward.

"The two most important days in your life are the day you are born and the day you find out why" – Mark Twain

I believe we are talking about life and death, maybe not right away, but over time physically, emotionally and spiritually as our passions and purpose get shoved further and deeper within ourselves. I believe we have a great responsibility for the overall well-being and livelihood of ourselves. If we are not living we are dying, there is no in-between or plateau. We are either growing or receding. If we look at time as a gift not to be taken for granted, but also not to be hurried through, then we can gracefully journey into the faithful and patient pursuit of ourselves.

We can then move forward with confidence continuing the process of becoming our true selves. The most wonderful and magical journey of becoming inspired for our greater purpose can lead us to depths unknown.

In this journey the hope is we can discover our passions and purpose, for this will propel us towards fulfillment. I'm not talking about the passions and purpose that get us noticed or recognized, although people naturally are attracted to this level of authenticity. What we seek is the kind of passions and purpose that shape us into exactly who we were meant to be. We seek a purpose that instinctually guides us to live each and every day committed with conviction, fulfilled and at peace, regardless of our present circumstances, knowing deep down there is a masterfully designed reason for where we are in this moment.

CHAPTER 2

The KEY to SUCCESS

What does it mean to you?

In order to find happiness, at some point in our lives, we need to honestly figure out what is our true definition of "success"?

We need to define this for ourselves, not how the world defines success.

At some point in our history the idea of success started to change from the continued progress of building our character into the mentality of building our own personal assets and status. Not allowing anything to get in the way of our "passions" was viewed as ambition. Pursuing and rationalizing success against all odds, even if we hurt people along the way, was normalized as determination or an accomplishment.

Can you imagine how much more value life would have if we defined success by how much we can build our character? What if we always did the next right thing, regardless of how hard it might be?

Honesty is the key. I think it's one of the traits that is lacking these days in our secular society. People rationalize being dishonest at times. But I think the most disturbing truth is we are dishonest with ourselves. We need to strive to be more honest with ourselves and what we believe in.

What brings true value to your life?

Let's start by defining success with what brings value to our life and the lives of others we encounter along our journey. If we start defining success by these standards, I believe we can change the world.

We cannot allow others to define what success should look like for us. If we are honest with our own definition of success, we will find we feel more purpose driven.

My quest for purpose developed through experiences. College became the host to a multitude of experiences of my journey, but the seed was planted well before it started growing on campus.

When I was a young kid, I was inspired by the culture, atmosphere and energy I felt while I was tagging along on a college visit with my mom, dad and older sister. My sister is a great singer and she was auditioning for a scholarship singing in the college's choir. What I felt and observed on campus expanded my world, showed me so many possibilities and planted a seed in my mind. I still remember the tour, the classrooms, the college students, the stained glass windows in the church...I knew from that moment I wanted to go to college someday.

Around that same timeframe in my life, my mom brought me down to the Houston area to visit family. As part of the trip we drove to the college my godmother worked at the time. I vividly remember the lawns in front of the buildings which were filled with people. Happy and joyful looking people, fit, fun and energetic people, passionate and purpose filled people, and these memories firmly stuck in my mind. There were cheerleader squads flipping around, hippies flinging Frisbees, lovers kissing on the grass, a book club sitting under the shade tree and a small environmental protest all taking place within a few blocks...the question wasn't why would I want to go to college it was why wouldn't I want to go to college!

One of the other reasons I went to college because it seemed like a good logical choice. I saw where the majority of people ended up that didn't go to college and those who did. People who went to college seemed successful and happy. Parents seemed to be so proud of the kids that went to college.

But I'm going to be honest; the greater reason was I wanted to feel that energy again. It seemed like an adventure that I couldn't pass up. The seed was planted many years prior as a young ten year old, as absorbed that energy and excitement on those college visits.

There was a sense of pride and duty to take advantage of the opportunity to go to a four year university. I was also fortunate to be recruited for playing football. I thoroughly enjoyed the simple small town which hosted the first eighteen years of my life, but I needed to enlarge my horizons. I felt college would be a much more fitting host for the next phase of finding my passion and purpose.

It is so interesting to me to think about a seventeen or eighteen year old trying to choose their career. We have only been able to think as "adults" for a short time and we are expected to pick a thirty to forty year career? Somedays I still don't know what I want to be when I grow up.

I was good at math and had a charismatic math teacher in high school, so I started college as a math major. But early on, I knew there was something else pulling at me, there was so much to explore and learn. It took three semesters, and then one day on my way from class walking back to the dorms I had an awakening. I was trying to figure out this algebra problem in my head throughout the day. On the sidewalk nearing the cafeteria I finally solved it; I still remember the exact spot. All of a sudden I realized I had floated through the day not engaging or interacting with a single person. I was in my head all day. I didn't connect to the people or the world around me at all. I am optimistic about the human race, I have to be, and enjoy people and interacting and building relationships. I also love to observe and connect with the beautiful intricacies that the cosmos breathes into the life around us. I was good at math, but this was not what I wanted to be doing day in and day out and it really wasn't bringing me true happiness or fulfillment. I wasn't connecting with people and the environment around me.

If we do things just because we are good at them, we may end up having a pretty solid career. We may be able to pay our bills and live out a pretty good life, but for me, I feel fortunate that I realized that I wanted more than that. I didn't want to have a job that attempted to fund my happiness; I wanted a job where I could be filled with passion and purpose 24/7. I wanted a life that provided me with a sense of purpose each and every day.

Ironically at the same time, I was taking an introductory recreation management class. The professor was so happy and positive and I was attracted to the passion he lived with each and every day. He was also very excited and supportive when I had an idea to make a video for a class project instead of writing a paper.

Honestly, I just wanted to drive around Wisconsin and go to festivals and brat fry's and have fun. I thought if I could somehow make a short film instead of writing a paper that would be awesome. I ended up putting more time into it than I thought. I felt plugged into the process and took it seriously because it was enjoyable and it felt like an adventure. I downloaded background music, edited the videos and interviews in the computer lab on campus.

The due date for the class paper came. As all the students in the class begrudgingly turned in their papers with no emotion on their face, I wheeled the TV in to show my film. This caught the attention of most of my classmates. They started to snicker and mumble about what the heck I was doing and how I was totally screwed because I didn't do the paper. I pressed play and the short film: "Wisconsin Summers" started to play. The others students watched in confusion as Jay-Z serenading the background music and some creatively edited footage of Wisconsin summer festivals played all of about 5 minutes, or 1/288th of my day. When the film ended there was a moment of silence.

"THAT'S WHAT I'M TALKING ABOUT!" shouted the professor.

He went on to say how this is the type of creativity that not only is what this profession needs but this world needs. When we think outside the norm we can take the ordinary to the extraordinary. Not only was it fun, I received an A and my fellow classmates were upset because as they spent their time typing, I was out enjoying the journey. I have to be honest that I took pleasure in being unique. I was hooked and found my new college major and profession. More importantly, it validated that it was ok to think differently and be uniquely myself.

That was years ago, and although I found a profession I am passionate about, I still struggled at times with what life means and if I was doing all I could do. No matter how far we've come in this journey, we all have times when we question why. If we look at this in the right perspective, this questioning is good. But we have to be committed to growth.

What more can I do?

Where do I fit into this vast world?

What is my overall purpose?

Sometimes I feel like I can conquer the world. Other times I feel as if the world is full of random noise and distractions. I feel like I'd be better taking a year off to become a monk. I could practice writing, fasting and chanting. Then when I come back it would all make sense or, even scarier, leaving wouldn't make any difference at all. In the past, I wouldn't share these feelings because of what people might think or how they might react.

We must be willing to accept our feelings in order to accept ourselves.

One day, while eating lunch with our priest, I opened up about these struggles.

He said, "Maybe you have a restless soul; actually maybe you've been gifted with a restless soul. It sounds like you are the type of person that has the ambition to continue to utilize this feeling to grow and continually develop yourself to make the world a better place."

His holy and positive perspectives on describing my urges as a blessing instead of a curse, like something was wrong with me, made me feel grateful.

We've all been instilled and given a gift by a power greater than ourselves. I wouldn't be paying respect to the life I've been blessed with by not utilizing this gift. The way this spiritual guide described it filled me with a spirit that the quest is the platform and to share my message is part of my purpose.

We need to be honest and share our struggles and triumphs with others. Everyone has pains, struggles and fears…it's a way to relate and connect with others.

As soon as anyone of us is perfect we have no useful purpose in this world. There was only one person who was perfect and he died on a cross of criticism.

Sharing your life with someone is the light which inspires others to use their gifts to the greatest potential.

The traits we thought were negative were only negative because we viewed them that way.

With this new point of view, you can then put on your positive lenses and use this knowledge and power to change. We are unstoppable if we are connected to our spirit. It's our responsibility to prioritize and take the time to develop it. Our spirit can lead us through anything if we trust it because it is a part of us and we are a part of it. We are one in the same. If our minds and hearts have a spirit of trusting in the best outcome we will have the best outcomes. There is nothing to fear. We will only be fearful of what we tell ourselves we are afraid of.

My goal is to live each day in touch with this divine power that drives me to be my best self and to enthusiastically serve others with purpose and passion.

Eckhart Tolle describes enthusiasm as, "…when we are flying through the air towards the target like an arrow, but enjoying every moment of the ride".

This type of enthusiasm ebbs and flows and might not last forever. We need to learn to be conscious and awakened to ourselves and our own mind. We need to understand how it works in us.

Become aware of yourself.

With every outward process or energy filled creative explosion there will also be an opposite inward moment. The Ying and Yang of life is a profound principle.

That's why we need to have our inner purpose be the engine for providing the energy we utilize every day. When we have a calm, balanced, focused, positive inner purpose it fuels any outer reactions. We can then respond with reason, confidence and the faith that everything in life will work out exactly the way it is supposed to.

It's in the seeking that we will find what we are looking for. The more we invest in improving in the knowledge of our self and what we are passionate about the more clear our passion and purpose will be and the more they will grow.

CHAPTER 3

PASSION

Discovering, reigniting and activating your passion can give the world and your life new meaning. It has gotten me through a lot of times in which I found myself struggling and questioning pretty much everything.

How do we live life to the fullest, love what we are doing and love people with an unwavering passion?

It all starts with loving ourselves.

There is a big difference between imagination and creativity.

I've always had an active imagination and a creative mindset. Einstein summed up how I feel when he said, "Imagination is greater than knowledge, knowledge is logical but imagination will bring you around the world." He went on to say, "The intuitive mind is a sacred gift and the rational mind is a faithful servant. We have created a society that honors the servant and has forgotten the gift." Interestingly, Einstein also found his world changing insights not in rational, linear thoughts but in a process he described using terminology called transcendence. Now, imagine how different the world would be if Albert Einstein would have only dreamed or imagined his ideas and not acted on them. To create you have to take action.

Please don't forget to be playful and have fun. Your spirit is only as healthy as you nurture it and give it the opportunity to be what it is meant to do...which is to soar.

How do you act? What do you do to better yourself and nurture your dreams daily?

Our youth learn from watching us and listening to adults, hearing and feeling our words. Monkey see, Monkey do. Such a simple saying we've heard since childhood, but true to this day. Like I said before, it's not what you do it's how you do what you do.

"There are no accidents" – Master Oogway

Purpose can happen sometimes by what seems like an "accident". The inventor of the Slinky got the idea by "accident". Richard James invented the Slinky in 1943, as he was working to devise springs that could keep sensitive ship equipment steady at sea. After accidentally knocking some samples off a shelf, he watched in amazement as they gracefully "walked" down instead of falling.

It may have been accidental, but it's up to us to be aware and act in these moments. We can perceive things as "accidents" or unique coincidences in which a different result is possible. I find it interesting to think about how different Richard James and so many others life's and purposes changed the world. How different his world could have been if he would have reacted differently to this apparent "accident". Over 300 million Slinkys have been sold as of 2005.

Yes, sometimes we stumble into our passions and purpose but most of the time it takes time, energy and hard work. We also need an awareness to understand our passions and how to utilize and share our purpose with the world around us.

Whatever you're trying to accomplish will be attainable. But you must study it, learn and relearn it. Submerge yourself in your passions and continually stride to improve yourself and you too will be "successful" in time. It's like working out to get more fit, studying for a degree or being looked at as an expert in your chosen profession, it takes time and effort. Rome wasn't built in a day, and unless you're one of the fortunate people who falls into it by accident, your passion and purpose will take dedication and persistence to develop. You have to define your own meaning of being successful, and like your principles and values, it will continue to morph and refine over time as will your purpose.

From a very young age, I was always persistent when I wanted something, I would go to any length to get it if it meant enough to me.

Each lesson we learn, good or bad, builds upon the next.

When I was a teenager, I got my first real job, besides picking rocks and bailing hay on my uncle's farm. I recently had turned sixteen years old and my parents encouraged me to get a job at the local grocery store. When I initially went up to the small hometown store they said they did not have any openings at that time. The next week I asked again. Rejection or failing was not in my vocabulary when I wanted something. My Dad and Mom said anything worth getting takes persistence and you have to work to get it. One of my friends worked there and I asked if he could put in a good word for me. At the same time, I went up to the store, once again, and kindly asked if they had any positions available as I was willing to start anywhere for any amount of hours and pay.

Just so happened, that day, someone just quit and they needed help. Doors open when you are prepared and take action.

You never know when purpose filled moments will happen. But I do know if you live life with passion, persistence and are prepared when they do your life will continue to exceed beyond your wildest imagination!

CHAPTER 3 PART II

PASSION = ENERGY

"Wherever your focus goes, energy flows" - Tony Robbins

I don't think passionate and successful people have endless amounts of energy, they just realize how and when to utilize it and what to spend their time focusing on. Less is more...or as my Grandma says, "Haste makes waste".

Do less of what draws energy away from you and do more of what gives you energy. Become aware of the things you are doing throughout your day and how much wasted time and energy goes into thoughts and actions that are not productive.

Our society is lacking the belief in the idea that our ability to make others around us better and more successful is a truest definition of success. The beauty of success is to bring people along for the ride. When your team is successful you will attract new and even more purposeful opportunities along the way. Think about great athletes who would have never even been discovered had they been on a losing team.

The key is to be prepared for the opportunity when it comes.

In high school, the end of my sophomore year came to a finish which meant a fun summer of baseball. Only problem was we only had one varsity team. We had no junior varsity team because of the lack of numbers of boys playing around our conference. For me this meant a fun summer of socializing, but probably no real meaningful time playing as there was at least one junior and senior ahead of me in the depth chart.

The first games of the season we had the opportunity to play in the stadium where the Minnesota Twins played. It was very exciting as it was an extremely different venue than we were used to coming from a small town.

As some of my best friends and I walked up the stairs from the locker room into the expansive venue chills went down my arms as I realized how small I was compared to the vast stadium. It probably helped ease any tension of playing there as all of our fans filled about four rows of seats, along with the fact that I would probably be watching the game, for the most part, from the bench.

The first game started and as I watched I noticed the lights and white roof gave the outfielders some trouble. The first couple pop flies were catchable but where dropped by the left fielder. Coach told the next player ahead of me in the depth chart to go in and he looked a little apprehensive but jogged out to left field the next inning. Now, I won't lie, subconsciously I was kind of hoping that the new left fielder would get a hit to him and he would drop it too…and before I could even finish my thought a line drive went screaming out to left field, just out of reach of the left fielders glove, and rolled all the way to the fence, which was over 400 ft. away. We were used to about 300 ft. of outfield depth and this caused the runner to get an in the park homerun.

In the moment of frustration, coach barked over to me to get out there, maybe I can catch a ball…and there was the moment I was patiently and persistently waited for! But in order for that opportunity to become reality I had to be ready and show up!

To make a long story short, I caught 4 balls that game with no drops, went 4-4 batting with my own in the park homerun and secured a starting spot on the baseball team for the next 3 seasons. I finished my senior year with a batting average of over .500, which may have never been possible if I was not prepared when the opportunity presented itself.

My sons are in Boy Scouts. One of their favorite times and mine is when we get to go camping. The first time we learned how to build a fire they were stoked, no pun intended. When you build a fire, what do you need? You need heat, fuel and oxygen. If you try to pile too wood on the fire it either smolders or burns up quickly and doesn't become sustainable. Similarly, if you stoke the fire too much it could go out.

It is much better to be really great at one thing than good at many. It is better to focus our efforts on what we are meant to be then to try to do too much or be the best at something you're not! As we strive to be the best at something we need to be aware there is never a finish line. No matter how much time and energy we put into any one thing there is always more to discover.

Leo Buscaglia described it simply, "If you are a banana than be the best BANANA you can be, if you try being a PLUM, it may be a really sweet and scrumptious plum, but you will always be second best no matter how hard you try!"

Don't listen or react to others who try to bring you down or crush your dreams. Some people will inherently try to bring you down from your cloud, but don't let them. If it is in you, part of you or it's something you're thinking, you may not understand it at the time but it is supposed to be there.

Nothing is impossible, it just might not have happened…yet.

Think about our smart phones. Which are little handheld computers that help us effortlessly communicate, receive e-mails and download presentations…it seems like a dream or science fiction. This was made possible because people dreamed and believed in the impossible.

Why have we lost that sense we had when we were a child to believe anything is possible? A couple of decades ago if I would have pulled a phone out of my pocket, opened it up and talked to another person across the globe, I would have either been seen as a genius or a god. When we stop believing anything is possible our dreams become impossible and we limit our ability to achieve greatness. Humans were made to be creative and strive for greatness.

Embrace your dreams, your imagination, your creativity... without fear, and start to understand how to utilize that feeling within yourself which can produce an inner energy that is beyond limits and expectations. Listen to your heart and don't always assume that an uncomfortable feeling is a "bad" thing. Instead treat it as motivation that something needs to be addressed.

When you start to change your perspective on these feelings and utilize them as a basis for personal growth you are on the path of discovering a breakthrough into something deeper. Big breakthrough moments in my life usually started out with an inner resistant or uncomfortable feeling. I had to choose to be brave and push through those feelings for on the other side there was great rewards.

What is truly you and what is not?

This answer lies within us. It becomes clearer through learning and growing from our life experiences and of trying over and over and over again. The Buddhist bumper sticker says, "Born again...and again and again and again". We inevitably are always coming back to the now, the present, and then we get to try again!

CHAPTER 4

PURPOSE

What is your Purpose?

For most people, it's not as easy or simple as you might think to answer this question.

We have all met purposeful and passionate people. You know the people I'm referring to; you know when they have it because you can feel it. They live it each and every day. They seem to have it all figured out. There is a natural attraction around them and we find that even if we don't necessarily agree with them we respect them because they live life with conviction.

Only we can honestly discover our true inner passion, no one can do this for us. Our purpose needs to be profound, to us. If it is, we will not need acceptance from others. It's how we utilize our passion to help others that will bring our passions to the level of purpose.

Each one of us is uniquely and perfectly made solely to fulfill our purpose.

This journey to find my purpose started when I started awakening to who I was and who I honestly wanted to become. When I stopped lying to myself and became willing to listen to the answers and take action, my life started to change. I started to realize that life was more than what I did or what I had. What was more important in the big picture was what I am capable of becoming.

A few questions to take the first step in discovering my purpose were questions like:

Who am I?

Who am I meant to be?

Why am I here?

Early on in my life, I thought, when I boiled everything down... as long as I was loved and happy, I felt that the rest of my life would just work out. All of my deep questions, contemplation and wonderment would be ok, as long as I felt good.

As we proceed through life, the definition of love and happiness and our interpretation of its definition changes. If we don't change with it we may struggle. Our experiences with love and happiness will be transformed and become richer if we view these natural changes as opportunities to grow in love and happiness. We cannot always see the magic of why certain things need to take place the way they do. But, I do feel from my experience, if we continue to pursue the journey we will find that everything happens as it was supposed to. We can either view every event as helping us draw closer to or further away from our own purpose.

But at some point, we will need to make a decision.

"We either make a decision to view the world as a positive or hostile world." – Einstein

If we trust in the essence and spirit of our inner truth then we will find peace in knowing that often times it's beyond our understanding.

"The way we respond to everything that happens in our lives causes us to either love more or love less." - Matthew Kelly

From a very early age, I felt like I was more empathetic than my peers. I really loved life and I loved people. I focused on the positive and had an optimistic outlook on life. I was a dreamer and saw the world through a different lens. As we grow older, life has a way of showing us a different truth, if we choose to believe it.

The only thing that is a guarantee is constant change. Life changes and you either can change with it or fight it against it. We have all had moments and periods in our life that have tested our resolve. I've had periods of my physical, mental and spiritual growth where I've had my perspectives and values tested. I didn't see it at the time, but I'm grateful now to have those experiences. If not for those experiences, I might not have pushed myself to grow better and instead I would have kept growing bitter. In hindsight, those times that tested my resolve, also forced me to learn new methods of finding and nurturing my inner happiness. These "tests" if life led me to rediscovering and transforming my purpose into reality.

In reality, the process of transformation is shaped daily. I started to realize I needed to wake up daily and direct my thoughts, intentions and actions to what I need to become instead of what I think I want or what anyone else thinks I should be.

We were all instilled with God-given gifts when we were created. Our purpose and God's gift to all of us is to be truly loved and fulfilled. Figuring out how to utilize these gifts for which we were created and share them with others makes all the difference in living a passion and purpose filled life.

I'm not saying to quit your job, although that's almost how I reacted once, but start to work towards doing the things that fulfill you and make you feel inspired. Starting today you can begin the process to reignite your dreams and the passion and purpose are hidden within you. Uncover the layers and start to reprioritize your life.

Maybe for you its woodworking, working on cars, reading, listening to good music, cooking, dancing, traveling, making people coffee, taking care of animals, kayaking, making origami, joining a club, starting a garden or whatever you feel an urge to do...start doing more of what you enjoy doing and what makes you happy in your free time.

Knowing ourselves and what makes us feel productive, motivated and inspired is worth the effort.

Some of us get energized by spending time with people; some of us need some time to ourselves. What makes you feel productive? What do you like doing? What makes you feel alive, connected and inspired? What would you do if you could do anything? Maybe you're lost and you don't even know what you like anymore.

Do you feel lost or stuck? There are so many people that have felt exactly like you, I know I have. You can start today by doing simple things that create positive change in your life. There are endless resources to get you started. There are Libraries full of books, YouTube videos, professional services and everyday people willing to help. It just takes one choice today and it can be the start you need to continue or expand your passion and purpose.

This book is meant to spark some thoughts and ideas to try and push you to go out there and resurrect your dreams, passions and purpose. Creating healthy habits like journaling, exercising, sleeping, meditating or writing a daily gratitude list are just some examples of daily practices, if you take action on, that will add more depth and dimension to your life and help you grow. When you're developing these qualities daily, your overall purpose will continue to become clearer along with what you were put on this earth to do.

I was on an airplane on my way to make a presentation at a conference with the theme, "Soaring to New Heights". My son just reminded me of this the other day as he spoke about the crystal clock they gave me for making the presentation and I started to think about one of the most impactful parts of that trip. As I settled in for the two and a half hour flight I decided to open up my notes to look over my presentation. In the single seat next to me sat a very ordinary and natural looking middle aged lady. She had long course gray hair and wore thick bottle cap glasses. She was wearing a knit sweater and no make-up. I couldn't really concentrate so I asked her where she was going, not anticipating the answer I received.

She said she was traveling to Australia to be the keynote speaker for a knitting conference. Her expertise was knitting items made from alpaca wool and she was invited to be the keynote speaker at an international conference in Sydney, Australia. I felt a little sheepish or should I say "alpaca-ish". Here I thought I was going to be the intriguing one, going to my state conference to make a presentation, but instead it turned out to be a humbling and great learning moment. She was so intriguing and filled with confidence, integrity and steadfastness knowing exactly what her purpose was as she humbly shared her passion with the world. How she got there was even more inspiring. She went on to tell me about how years ago she wrote down ten goals that she was going to accomplish and how she proceeded to set out to achieve them.

One of her goals was to have her alpaca clothes worn by a model in a modeling runway show, which she already accomplished. Another was to have her craft be recognized internationally, which she was on her way to do. I learned a couple valuable lessons during that flight. One was we shouldn't pre-judge people. Another lesson was when you find something you love doing, set goals and take action. No matter how big your goals are you can accomplish them as long as you are focused, willing and determined. She will never realize how she gave me the inspiration for the session I was going to present during that conference and also how she taught me some valuable life lessons in that random moment on the plane. She reminded me to never lose sight of my inner purpose and passion, always dream big, set goals and then go out there and try to achieve them.

"Awakening as a future event has no meaning because awakening is the realization of Presence" - Eckhart Tolle

Your purpose will become much clearer the more you can become aware. Start by slowing down, breathing and practicing being present and participate in being an active part of your own transformation. You will make a greater impact in the world around you by unlocking your passions. Once you unlock your passion and let it loose your purpose will become clearer. When people unleash their purpose the people and the world around them also change.

Try not to react to your first thoughts or emotions, although they are there for a reason, the key is to become aware of them and start to grow in knowledge and understanding of how they are currently present in your life.

There were times in my life where I thought I should just drop everything and become a merchant marine or a treasure hunter and set sail around the world. I'm glad I took a few slow deep breaths and did the right thing as that would have definitely changed the course of my journey and the impact it would have had on many others close to me.

Taking time to slow down and practice living in the moment allows me to follow my soul's direction for my life. I find inner peace and happiness in the present moment. Instead of thinking I'm going to find happiness from material or worldly things, when I slow down and live in the moment, my soul lets me know its ok to be myself. My spirit reminds me to accept my present circumstance as being exactly how they are supposed to be at this time in my life. It reminds me fulfillment isn't found in worldly possessions or in distant lands. It doesn't matter where I am or what is happening in my life, I can handle it

37

with grace and understand that everything I go through leads me even closer to my true purpose. To discover my true purpose I have to look within...or I might forever be without.

CHAPTER 5

PARTAKE IN AN ABUNDANT LIFE

The 1/288th rule

Miracle Minutes

Throughout this book make sure to write down your thoughts, goals and dreams and what inspires you. This will help you define your goals as you pursue your purpose.

Everyone is different. Each of us have different definitions and levels of achievement we strive for which we think will make us feel "successful". Our fast paced media driven society likes to give us the definition but the truth is we are all meant for our own unique purpose. If we look within ourselves instead of comparing ourselves to others our purpose and passion will give us the power to accomplish almost anything we set our minds to. No one ever made a difference by being the same as everyone else.

One of the most important ways you can partake in this process is by being an active participant in this journey called life.

One day I was in the driveway waiting for everyone in my family to get ready and in the car. Between my five kids and a wife, there is always someone that takes longer to get in the car than expected. I used to get frustrated and inpatient, but I became aware one day that the only person that it seemed to bother was me. Upon examining this phenomenon with my reactions in other predicaments in my life I found that in most situations when I was frustrated the only person that seemed bothered was me.

I started to realize that I was wasting this time. I was wasted miraculous moments. Instead of being inpatient and getting upset I started to discover ways to maximize this time. These five minute intervals throughout my day started to add up and brought me richness and added value to my life. Instead of grumbling and complaining about why it's taking so long for these things to happen I prepared for these moments and utilized this time to grow myself and nurture healthier relationships.

I don't always get a lot of time to spend with my kids during the week so when I have five minutes to interact with them I love to maximize this time. Instead of sitting there getting frustrated we would do things like grab a basketball and we would shoot a lot of baskets in the hoop at the end of the driveway while we waited. I put a football in the car and during those moments where we might be waiting on someone; my son would run a couple post routes. It's as easy as picking a subject to talk about or watching an ant carry a bug twice its own size and discuss how strong the ant and your own child is!

Do you realize the power these impactful moments can make?

These moments can change our world! It's amazing how wonderful your mood can instantly change by turning on a good song and dancing like you're in a "Dancing with the Stars" competition with your daughter for five minutes. The best part is most songs are about four to five minutes and dancing is also good exercise. The exercise alone gets your heart beating and makes you feel good. Now think about how your mood changes when you're listening to a great song, add that to dancing with your son, daughter, grandson, granddaughter, wife, husband or heck, all by yourself…and you just changed the course of your entire day. I believe these moments will change the world!

My wife was getting ready to go one Saturday morning and in

the five to ten minutes of transition time I couldn't believe how much I accomplished. I took some stuff down to the basement, helped my son grab a board game, turned on the radio quick and danced with my daughter around the basement swinging and swooping her around like she was a princess and even got in a few quick shots on the basketball hoop with my other son. It's amazing how simple it is to turn those transition times from frustration to celebration and it only takes five minutes, $1/288^{th}$ of your day.

My goal is to take all those five minute miracles and intentionally partake in living during those moments. These five minute moments become miracles. Instead of wasting this time or getting agitated, we can start to utilize it by asking people how their day went, writing in our journal, or reading that inspirational book we keep neglecting. It's as easy as keeping a positive book, CD or brain game in the glove box to pull out when we have an extra couple minutes.

These miracle minutes will add up and will become an intuitive part of your day! They may seem to be insignificant moments throughout our day, but when your daughter comes up to you and says, "I felt like I was flying through the air when we were dancing", well, who doesn't want to fly through the air! It never would have happened if I had not purposefully taken advantage of those five minutes of our day.

The other thing that happens when we take action and maximize those five minutes is it motivates us and builds momentum for more success. Whether it's a work project, cleaning the house, working out or picking up that phone to see how someone's day went, it's taking the first step that makes all the difference.

Within minutes of a workout at the gym or at home, all of a sudden my adrenaline starts pumping, the sweat starts to roll down my brow and I start to feel my body loosen up. Before you know it I have thirty minutes in and I'm feeling great for the rest of my day. At home when I'm staring at that yard work I've been putting off or that window that needs repair, it's the first five minutes that are the hardest.

Five minute intervals over time, add up. Take five minutes during commercials to get something done, do some sit-ups, read a quick book to your child. Five minutes a day for 365 days adds up to over 30 hours of year of positive change! Imagine if everyone took these five minute miracles and added them up...I'll let you do the math on that one. But truly this is why I believe these miracle minutes can change the world!

Now, start intentionally thinking about how many five minute miracle moments are in your day that you can partake in. Showing up five minutes earlier for work, waiting for your wife to get ready, picking up your kids from practice...you can easily see how those $1/288^{th}$'s of your day can add up.

All it takes is five minutes to start to build success and personal growth and change our life from ordinary to extraordinary.

For me, success is more about character building and actively participating in life and less about what I can accumulate or who or what I can benefit from along the way.

Develop a Productive Process for Progress.

The definition of "PROGRESS" is a series of actions or steps taken in order to achieve a particular end.

There is no "end game" there are only new "beginnings" and once you find your purpose and passion the energy and profound impact you have in this world will be limitless!

Businesses or organizations that implement processes that are effective, efficient and address problems with solutions become successful. Businesses that find a process that works can then duplicate that process over and over again making it seem like there is no limit to the amount of people and profits that they can influence. When you add passion and purpose filled employees into organizations that have successful processes they become world changing businesses.

Fast food chains; once they find a process that works, can infiltrate pretty much any and all cities. It works because their process gives them what they are looking for in a fast, affordable and effective way. With any process there are pro's and con's, and with fast food, we start to settle for what is comfortable, fast and easy. It serves a purpose but then we feel sluggish, fat and empty. Our country loves fast food, and I will admit, every once and a while I do to because I don't feel like I have the enough time or can wait. We have an obesity probelm and its because those five minute intervals we are waiting in that fast food line is adding up. Those minutes add up too and are slowly killing us. We need to plan ahead and be a little more creative about the produce we consume.

Part of why fast food is such an easy option is we think we need to fill our days with as much as possible. This causes more struggle because we are so busy all the time. We don't even take the time to make good meals or sit at the dinner table as a family anymore. We need to slow down and live more simply.

Life is Simple...but not easy!

"Live simply so others may simply live." St. Mother Theresa

When I simplify my life my life becomes simple. When it becomes too simple I start to feel like I'm bored or the day to day routine gets monotone and lacks excitement or spontaneity. This forces me to change or settle and the cycle continues. This awareness of how this cycle affects my happiness day to day has forced me to understand that I need to continually evolve and be aware of my happiness each and every day. When I focus on living each day the best I can this process is a positive experience instead of a daily struggle.

How do we get better at something? We take a lot of little steps over and over towards a goal. Stop looking outward and start looking inward and take the first step. Start to create a plan and take part in your own individual process. Each day will add up that you make an effort to better yourself. Before you know it a week, a month and then a year will go by. Then take time to look back and see the progress. Don't forget about the past, just don't dwell on it. The only way to see how far you've come is to look back at where you were. You will be at the very same point or worse if you don't start now. Just make a decision that someday is today!

I've written in my journal for many years. Prior to five years ago I was very inconsistent but dedicated myself towards writing more consistently recently. Then came the weekend where I got sick of saying someday I'm going to write a book, and I made a decision. One Saturday morning I grabbed a cup of coffee and sat down to read through and organize the last sixteen years of my journals. It was eye opening to become aware of the progression and process my life went through over the years.

The first journal I wrote as an adult was about nine days of me writing and then it stopped. The next entry was about a year later. There were sporadic blips of entries, poems or random experiences with the best of intentions but it was in about year twelve or thirteen before it became a daily practice. No wonder I made no real growth. Until I started the process of intentionally dedicating the time to practicing journaling daily, noticing any kind of change or measuring tangible growth was difficult.

I bet anything it won't take sixteen years to see the progress if you are committed to a healthy practice like journaling. You will be amazed in as little as a month or two how your perspective and attitude on daily life can change. You will discover a lot about yourself and become more aware of your thoughts and feelings. It's also very enlightening and helpful to be able to look back and see your growth. Maybe for you it's not journaling, maybe it's eating healthy, exercising or learning how to play guitar? The key is to be open to start something and try new methods to learn and become awakened to what processes work for you.

You will need to set aside a dedicated time. This may be different depending on what stage you are at in your life and what your current schedule looks like. Right now, for me, mornings are the most important part of my day. My morning routine or ritual of waking up and getting my mindset towards positive thinking, gratitude and living the best I can that day makes all the difference in how my day goes. This last year, with five kids, ages eleven down to nine months, I have had my fair share of struggles getting up earlier to devote to an early morning self-care practice. But without fail, every time I did get up and take action, I had a better outlook for the day and how I reacted to the events that took place in it.

This one "process" or habit of waking up and being devoted to a morning routine of prayer, reflection, physical exercise and meditating on positive readings has made such a huge difference in my life. It made such a difference it propelled me to take action to share my story with others! Once I got through the initial struggle and shock of waking up early and committing to the routine it became something I looked forward to. It actually made me want to go to bed earlier at night because I looked forward to that time in the morning. You can start with intervals, waking up five minutes earlier each day over the course of a week or two, but I'm a rip off the Band-Aid kind of guy.

I started waking up at least thirty minutes earlier, and then quickly realized an hour earlier each day was even better. I got myself taken care of first so I could better take care of others. I felt more plugged into the stream of life. I forced myself to think about what I could give back to life instead of what I could take from it. I practiced becoming other-centered instead of my natural inclination to be self-centered. Before my feet even hit the ground, I start by thanking God for another day. It is a scientifically proven fact that investing in positive thoughts during the first five minutes after you wake up dramatically improves your mindset throughout the day. Once again, it's not a question of why would you fill those five minutes with positive thoughts, its why wouldn't you fill them with gratitude and positivity?

On those days when I feel like I have to peel myself out of my warm blanket it may be a struggle but I know the result. I sometimes need to take a moment and change my perspective. Instead of saying, "I have to…do this or that today", it becomes, "I get to and am grateful for being able to get up and grab our youngest daughter from her crib." How dramatic that one word changes my entire outlook by changing "have to" to "get to". As I brought our littlest daughter out of her crib and put her down alongside me, I needed to stay disciplined. Even if it's only five to ten minutes of positive readings and saying my prayers and a quick three to five minute yoga stretch to get my mind, soul and body moving in the right direction. If it's just not possible that day, I choose that particular morning to be in the moment, just taking five minutes to be still and breathe and be present while holding her, she will never be this small again, she is such a miracle.

A morning routine makes all the difference. Find what works for you and make it as consistent as possible but also be open to magical moments like staring into your child's eyes as they examine your face with mystery. Just make sure whatever you do it is positive and you will be imprinting positive messages in your mind and soul. So maybe some days you can't afford thirty minutes or an hour, its ok, the important part is to keep the practice going. It will balance out.

The more time I have the better, but those miracle minutes add up and have such a great impact on my well-being.

There are literally thousands of books, quotes, inspirational messages that are available. There are also countless videos on YouTube or other venues to get your mind tuned into Passion and Purpose driven messages. What have you to lose, a couple minutes of sleep?

If you start with spending even the first five minutes of your day thinking positive and having an attitude of gratitude, which is only 1/288th of your day...it will be well worth it. It's proven by neuroscience and I testify it works if you commit to doing it!

CHAPTER 6

I AM

Even before Moses was told by the burning bush we have had the answer within us. God said, "I am what I am", and we too are what we say we are. The key is do we wholeheartedly believe it?

When I started this journey to find myself and what "I am" at age thirty-one, rediscovering my passion and purpose, I had gotten to the point where I didn't even believe what I was telling myself anymore. I had tried to tell myself for years that I was the best I could be. I kept telling myself the thoughts, behaviors and actions I had were normal and acceptable. I would compare myself to others and convince myself I was better off, even though deep down I didn't believe it. My ego and character defects needed to be addressed. I knew deep down what I was and what I wasn't. I was lying to myself. I needed to accept that I had to clear away my past resentments and relearn everything I thought I knew. Only then could I start to rebuild, become aware, and with the guidance of God, discover who I am.

My wife gave me a book written by Joel Osteen when I was struggling to rediscover my passion. In one of the chapters there is a simple but effective sentence, I am, followed by a positive affirmation, which has the ability to change how you think and feel about yourself. A simple practice, which may feel weird at first, but try it. Start the day by filling in this phrase. Throughout the day do the same thing.

I am _____.

Whatever you insert in this simple sentence you will become. This simple affirmation and what you insert in this simple sentence will determine what kind of life you will live. Your thoughts become your reality. I am blessed, I am strong, talented, beautiful, passionate, positive, loved, talented, prosperous, healthy, full of energy, confident, happy, a good listener, good at remembering names, and successful. The words you insert will bring you Gods blessings and favor. It's up to you to choose what follows the "I am." Some of us have a tendency to insert words that bring harm to ourselves and hinder our ability to grow. Never say negative things about yourself. For some reason when we are not in a good place we have no problem criticizing ourselves.

"I am." I believe these might be, along with what follows, the most powerful words in the English dictionary.

Little short affirmations can change your entire day. Like I said, it may feel weird at first, but give it time and you will find a rhythm that works for you.

"If you can't figure out your purpose, figure out your passion. For your passion will lead you right into your purpose." T. D. Jakes

I started to use this phrase when I was trying to unlock my passion and purpose. "I am passionate about _____." (Fill in the blank)

Another example of the power of these two words is rearranging how we use them. Rearranging these two simple words can change the intention from asking yourself to telling yourself what you are. Think about the life-changing difference it makes just by changing around the order of this short sentence.

Am I enough?

Now, change that to, **I AM ENOUGH!**

You are enough! We all have pains, struggles, shame...that hold us back. They hold us back from leading a life filled with the passion God made us to live for! We are held back from being vulnerable and sharing our true self with others. The choice between our minds saying, "Am I enough" to "I am enough", takes about the same amount of energy but has an incredibly different outcome in your daily life. "I am enough" fuels your passions and grows your purpose. "Am I enough" keeps you stuck in your head and in the thoughts that trap your passions from coming into the light. "I am enough" helps you accept and love yourself and look at your pain as a means to build character. Your life and others you share it with will take on new meaning.

When you are not vulnerable you give up the opportunity to have your depth and authenticity transform your purpose. When you are not vulnerable with others you give up the ability to change others' lives. We all deep down want a lasting legacy. We all deep down just yearn to be loved. Don't miss this opportunity to be vulnerable, transparent and authentic with others. Be the real you!

Don't worry about changing others. You can't change other people. People will only change when the pain of staying the same is greater than the pain of changing.

Some of you may feel selfish taking time for yourself. I was struggling with this thought until one day a friend told me to change my mindset from the perspective of being selfish to practicing self-care. What a different mindset I have and how much more present I can be for others if I take care of myself. It's like the airplane attendant that makes sure you know to put on your mask first before attempting to help others.

Just make a decision. The word decision is derived from "incision" or to cut-off...like cutting off a limb, its final, there is no going back. When you make a choice that is final like this you are willing to do whatever it takes to change. Cut the ropes on the boat and sail in a new direction! Most of the time we cut off the past or we say we are willing, but then we start to struggle or it gets difficult so we reach back out and grab the rope again. Don't give yourself the option. Make a decision and then intently move forward with action and commitment to improving, no matter what.

What holds you back?

Fear of failure, or death…well I hate to break it to you but we are all going to die. Knowing this is actually our greatest gift. It tells us that we better start living life to the fullest, doing what drives us, what makes us feel the most alive…we don't get a second chance, as far as I know.

Pope John Paul II said, "The sooner we can come to the realization that we all die the sooner we can stop taking life for granted and start living!"

Living your fullest life starts today!

Our world is created within us. The world we create within our mind becomes the world we live in. We have the ultimate, eternal and unlimited power to be more than we can even imagine is possible. What you say about yourself becomes who you are. It's not what others say about you, it's what you say about you that makes all the difference.

So who do you want to be?

What do you want to do?

What world are you going to live in?

Only you can ultimately determine the answers to these questions.

Someday is today, and you can start now, by filling in this phrase, "I AM _____."

CHAPTER 7

PRIORITIES

Whatever you make your priority, what you focus your efforts and mind on, will become your reality.

What if our priority was to be kind to others?

How would this change us and our world?

Invest in positive priorities and the results will show for themselves. How we feel and connect to others will take on new meaning. If you make happiness your priority, then I believe you will be happy. If you make others happiness your priority then I believe your life will take on new purpose. I believe this is how we can change the world! It seems counterintuitive but making others happy will lead you to a truly fulfilled and purposeful life.

Our priorities consume all of our time. Time is the most precious gift we have. Those who have lost a loved one or someone close to them can relate. I never want to be the person that says, "If only I had more time, or done this or that". Our time can run out in an instant when we least expect it. Whatever we invest our time naturally becomes our priority. When I'm struggling, it's usually because my priorities are not in line with my purpose. Our purpose isn't to invest our time in things that are negative or don't add value to our life and the lives of others.

We only have so much control in this life. Every day our priorities can change. Sometimes we change them, other times they are changed for us.

With five kids, my most feared season is flu season. About a month or two after the kids go back to school the Wisconsin air changes and the coolness of the northern country comes swooping down. It's inevitable that at least one in our tribe will bring something home with them. This forces the priorities of my day to change dramatically. There seems to be no time for any self-care or personal improvement, I feel like I'm barely getting through the day.

It's vitally important to realize you're exactly where you're supposed to be at that time. Try to stay grateful for your blessings, not your perceived curses; there is always someone that has it worse. Even when the world seems unfair, I force myself to think of the positives...like when my kids are sick, I say, they are building good immunity for the long run.

My mom said that when I was really young I would get sick quite a bit. She let me play in the dirt, run around without shoes on, play around my grandma and grandpas farm, climb around in the haymow, tromp through the woods and swim in the creek. I honestly can say, and evidence backs this up, because of all of the time I spent when I was young getting dirty and sick my immunities have built up and my adult life has been very healthy overall. This has allowed my priorities to change from paying attention to my health to paying attention to the health of my family. Sometimes you are allowed more flexibility in setting priorities because of experiences you already had.

Now, if we honestly look at our priorities, we will see that there are some good and some bad priorities. We each have character traits that are good and bad, if we were perfect then we would be God. We would have no use in this world and have nothing to work on and nothing to learn or share with others. The goal is to make our priority working to better ourselves, which is the only way we will continue to grow and have more to offer in this world. If we are truly honest during this process of finding our purpose and passion we will find love each and every day of life in the giving of ourselves.

The love that spreads from sharing our true selves, which is filled and fueled with the power of our purpose and passion, can leave a mark beyond this world and for many generations to come.

Another way to look at it...If you take a look at your checkbook or account ledger you will see there are credits and debits, and when the credits outweigh the debits then we are in good financial shape. You will have extra funds and are able to spend more on our priorities. How much more value would your life bring to this world if you spend your extra credits on your purpose and passions?

Sometimes our negative priorities build up and make it really difficult for us to overcome the deficit or it feels as if we are drowning in debt. This can be self-inflicted but a lot of times there are things beyond our control that contribute as well. We can't control what happens all the time but we can choose to control and become aware of how we react to it and what we do about it. We can grow better or bitter because of it.

This bodes even truer for our purpose and passion, if we work towards creating the habits that build our character the universe will answer and provide ample opportunities to reward us.

There is also power in saying "no". I used to have a hard time saying no, but sooner or later my yes's and my ego's thinking that I could to do everything and be superman for everybody became extremely counterproductive. This led to burnout, unhealthy habits and feeling even worse for not producing or having enough time or energy for the things and people that truly made my life whole.

The next time a situation or decision that doesn't quite feel right comes up or that you're not sure about, take a few calm breathes and it will become easier to answer with affirmation when you're calm. It's perfectly fine to say I'll have to think about that and get back to you. Not reacting has worked especially favorable when I'm discussing things with my wife or kids. I listen and take time to actually interpret how I feel and then discuss things in a loving and tolerant manner. This has made a world of difference in the everyday levels of peace in me and our household.

As you start to get more confident in what your priorities are and where your purpose is leading you it becomes a lot easier to make decisions and take advantage of opportunities when they arise. You will become confident and be prepared when opportunities present themselves.

"It's better to be prepared for an opportunity that doesn't happen then to have an opportunity and not be prepared". Les Brown

When I got my first big opportunity to speak at a national aquatic conference I was asked if I was willing to be the endnote speaker. I could have easily said no I'm not ready or I've never done that. It would have been a lot less stressful to just do a couple sessions and leave the endnote to someone else. But I said, "of course I can, I would love to share the power that having purpose and passion in our everyday lives can bring to each person, family, workplace and community."

It was almost a year away and I told myself, if I can't put together an hour long presentation on this subject in a year then maybe I shouldn't be doing this in the first place. Also, what's the worst that can happen, I present to 400 attendees and they leave saying this guy is a joke...they don't know me anyway! Throughout my experience, whenever you speak out with passion and purpose, you're always going to have some naysayers, so plan on it. I also believe that if I could truly make a difference in even one person's life than it would be worth the risk.

I believed in myself. I visualized myself as successful, impactful, and prepared. "I am a great speaker, I am a purpose driven and passionate person...I am born to do this!" I immersed myself in speaker tapes and explored the possibilities. I practiced what I preached and imagined it would be a great opportunity to change others' lives.

I spoke from the heart and in the weeks following calls and requests to speak at other conferences looking for a speaker with energy and passion just showed up. If people are looking for something different that was ok with me, all I can do is be me. I strived to extract my experience to help others and be the best I could be. When people truly give their best I believe the universe always rewards them accordingly.

CHAPTER 7 – PART II

Priorities become a personal quest

A big part of my overall wellness is working out. I love the adrenaline and endorphins I get after a good workout. I feel so much better and get so much more done throughout my day.

I'm a different person, for the better, when I get my body moving. At minimum, I feel at least 10-20 minutes of physical exercise, is essential to my well-being. I prefer to have 30-45 minutes of exercise, and a lot of days I do because I make it a priority. I always feel better throughout my day when I exercise. However, between getting our five kids ready and out the door for school, work, responsibilities and trying to find a couple minutes to let my wife know she is a precious gift in my life, it gets difficult.

The other morning I knew I had back-to-back meetings all day and didn't know if I would have time to get a workout in. As you know already I follow the 5 miracle minute rule (1/288th of your day) and always, at the very minimum, try to get 5 minutes in to kick start my day...after prayers and some positive readings. This specific morning I did a five minute new high impact workout, and man, I didn't know you could sweat so much and breathe so heavy in just 5 minutes...1/288th of my day. I was in our closet and I was breathing so heavy my wife asked me from the other room if I was ok. You need commitment and discipline and you will inevitably find out what works for you and within a short time you will start to see and feel progress and change.

I also love to eat. When I struggle with my weight or how I feel it's usually when my debits of eating too much or unhealthy outweigh my credits of working out or eating more vegetables. As I get a little older I also have to change it up to find the balance.

I was on a running kick for about four years when I started this journey into finding and reinventing myself. It really helped me calm down and hone my thoughts on what was important and leveled off any anxiety over things that didn't really matter. After pounding my back and knees 3 to 4 times a week over the course of over 200 weeks, I started to feel pains I never experienced before and had to slow down. I even went to the chiropractor. Like the pressure in a valve, too much or too often, without taking time to let out the steam it could cause our body to become overstrained. This can result in pain or, worse yet, if the pressure builds up in a valve too much it may even blow!

Not just physically, but also mentally and emotionally, I had built up the pressure in my system over the years without taking notice that the gauge was heading into the red zone. I had to modify my life and find a more balanced approach. I started practicing and blending yoga, high rep but low weight lifting, walking more in between runs, riding bike, playing with my kids, viewing vacuuming and raking leaves as a workout too and the list goes on. I became more aware of how my body and mind reacted and felt the day of and day after workouts. I discovered what balance allowed me to be at an optimal level of wellness. Listening to my mind and how my body felt helped me understand what was good for me.

Sharing our passions becomes a purpose when we share them with others. I wanted others to feel as good as I felt and I believe we have an obligation to share our gifts. At work this meant creating a health and wellness initiative called FIT in the Parks. We set up a series of free fitness classes throughout various parks and public spaces that brought people together and connected them through a common platform.

If we don't share and try to spread our love and passion it dies with us.

There are many instances in my life where circumstances could have been interpreted as the worst thing that could have ever happened to me.

When I was 21 years old, I bought a new motorcycle, and took off into the Amish countryside down the beautiful winding roads of highway 33. Just two days before the start of football training camp for a quick relaxing getaway. I loved every minute of the hot august sunshine on my face, thinking about how in a couple weeks I'd be catching touchdown passes.

Four exhilarating but short hours later, as the mid-august sun beat down on me, I found myself face down on the smoldering asphalt with a crushed right leg and road rash covering my body. I thought to myself, I wish I wouldn't have done that, but somewhere deep inside me I knew it would be ok, and I never gave up hope and the idea that everything has to happen for a reason.

After wallowing in self-pity for a couple weeks, I made a decision to utilize this time to slow down and concentrate on my studies, get my degree and enter "the real world". Funny how life has a way of balancing things out for us when we don't do it ourselves!

I was never really that interested in a "traditional" career path. Many years later, I found myself doing just that. As I sat in my comfortable corner office, I continued to feel there was so much more to explore. I just didn't realize that the journey was to explore and grow within.

One thing I did know is no matter where I was in my life or what I was doing I always felt alive and purposeful when I lived and worked with passion! When I truly thought and believed any-thing was possible and anything I could imagine could happen!

I made a choice to do just that, where I was at currently, and start growing and shaping myself and my position into an impactful community asset. I got out of the office more, submersed myself in the community. I made it a point to inter-act with people and build positive programs, partnerships and initiatives while focusing on building healthy relationships. I made connecting with others and building relationships a high priority. I made an effort to get involved and traveled to confer-ences to present and spread the news of the award winning pro-grams we were implementing.

While I grew the division and impacted the community in my day job, I never lost sight of my passions and my purpose, in the hopes of profoundly helping others even more. I realized what made me feel truly alive and connected was speaking and writing about my experiences and what I'm passionate about. I made a deep commitment to improving myself physically, mentally and spiritually. I also continued to dedicate time, even if it was just a little bit, to writing about my journey.

I always dreamt of becoming a writer. Although, at times my purpose and passion was subdued or I struggled to find out what it was or what it meant for me, I've always felt the urge. Anyone that accomplishes anything of significance has that inner urge!

I could have just settled for a pretty darn good day job, but in-stead, I started to invest in my passions and purpose even more. It didn't happen overnight but when you commit to making something a priority and believe it will positively impact your life and the lives of others around you, you will find joy and success.

I made my top priority to become the best version of myself and my outlook on life kept getting better.

My mission is to live each day believing that as long as I try my best, striving to be my best self, everything will work out for the best.

Honestly, what are your priorities and how do you invest in them?

How do you find balance?

When we are beginning to discover or rediscover ourselves, we have a hard time regulating our energy and focus.

Balance is essential and yet we overcomplicate it. I know at times I try to be everything for everyone as I have a tendency to be a people pleaser. What and how I felt about myself came from what others thought about me or how I thought they saw me. Throughout the years I've realized if I am living a life filled with passion and purpose it doesn't matter what others think about me. It's not important what others think about you, what's important is what you think about yourself!

I have the tendency to get caught up in the day to day. I forget about my own personal ambitions or put them on the backburner and my excuse is telling myself it's for the good of the whole so I don't need to do what drives me today. This not only hurts the whole, it's not honest, and eventually causes more pain in the long run. At some point, you will have to decide whether to accept your present circumstances or change. It took me many years and lots of inner and external struggles before realizing that I was the only person I could change and transform. Those around me could potentially benefit from the change or growth but the reality was my choices to change made a profound impact on me and how I felt, not necessarily on them. We can only change and transform ourselves. Whether or not other people decide to commit to true change is out of our control.

Once I started to become aware of how my body, mind and soul operated, it slowly became more apparent to me that I needed to exhaust less energy on those things that didn't bring me closer to my passions and purpose. I had to practice being more balanced. The ability to have equal levels of energy output and consumption will be the difference in whether or not your body and mind, or machine, runs at its most efficient level. Machines that run with high efficiency and effectiveness run with ease and minimal energy and effort expended.

If you overwork, overstress, over-commit you may think you finally have "it", but you may not have anything but a bunch of negatively charged emotions, ulcers, disappointed and confused friends or family around you. Unless you are aware of yourself and your actions and find ways to balance your life, you will not be truly fulfilled because you will not be able or aware to expend the energy needed when moments of real and lasting happiness come into your life.

CHAPTER 8

PRESENT

Being Present is the Present

Happiness takes place in the present moment. Fulfillment becomes present in our lives through millions of present moments over "time". Like a sculptor working on a striking piece of art, the moments slowly add up and start to shape and define who you are. We smooth out the rough parts of our life over time. Great and historically acclaimed masterpieces took time, patience, discipline and even faith.

You can insert any feeling or want in place of happiness. Success takes place in the present moment. Love takes place in the present moment. Lasting success and love shapes and transforms over time. Pain, struggle, worry, depression and anxiety also shape your reality over time.

If you are living in the past then you are going to be depressed from rehashing and thinking about things that you are unable to change. If you are living in the future you are going to be anxious worrying about things that may or may not happen. The only time you are truly living the most in control and the happiest is when you are living in the present moment.

Happiness comes down to your thoughts and how you react to the situations you are presented with. When you enhance your ability to live in the moment and not react negatively instead, responding with a positive spirit, your life will change dramatically and your happiness will soar.

Happiness and the joy of being truly fulfilled comes from within. Take the young child at Christmas who has to have that year's "It" toy, the newest clothes or video games. And you have the parent who is stressed out trying to run around to find and pay for it and you have multiplied the anxiety two fold which actually takes away from the joy of the holiday. Then when they receive the toy or designer clothes it brings them instant happiness and gratification. Both the child and parent feel good and happy in the moment as they have received and given a great gift. But deep down it does not bring either one of them fulfillment. It may make them feel happy, liked or popular for a short time, but this feeling quickly wears off and they are left with their true feelings, a toy that sits around not being played and a credit card bill waiting to be paid. These "things" that society tells us will make us happy never last and eventually we need to discover what makes us feel truly fulfilled. When we discover our passion and purpose we don't need the "things" that our media driven society tells us we need.

Want even more proof, some of the happiest people in the world went through the harshest situations imaginable.

I've always been intrigued by stories of people who have been through harsh circumstances and overcame them to live an inspiring life. Some were imprisoned, thrown against their will in concentration camps or born into some of life's most horrible circumstances, yet somehow, they have a profound peace within themselves and their surroundings.

Although drastically different situations, we can all relate to this in our daily lives as we all have challenges we face.

I was once faced with a circumstance at work where I was put into a leadership position in which one of my equal level colleagues now reported to me. That person was 30 years older than me and had been an employee of the organization for over 30 years. What made things difficult is this person performed a leadership role I was now assigned. To make a long story short, he made my new role extremely difficult and interactions with him were filled with "growth opportunities". I became filled with anxiety every time I had to meet or interact with him. It took some time and patience, but I chose to be present in the situation and started looking at this colleague as a great teacher. Every time I met or communicated with this employee, I started to train my mind to become aware of how I felt, and overcome and learn how to be a better leader with employees through difficult situations.

Our greatest fight is within our own minds. We may act or look like we are fine. But people have no idea the prison we may feel like we are in, inside our minds. We can feel trapped, full of fear, not able to make even a simple decision. If this is what is going on within you it is ok. You can overcome it. You are exactly where you are supposed to be at this very moment in life and there is hope. I believe in Divine Providence, it's what I choose at this moment in my life. Either everything happens for a reason or it's all just a series of random circumstances that mean nothing and lead to nowhere.

When we live in the moment and do the very thing we need to do in that moment everything else works out.

Some days there are so many things that I feel I have to do. It feels as if I'm pulled in a million directions. I had to learn how to stop and decide what I needed to do in that moment? As long as you're moving forward, no matter how little the progress, the best you can do is enough.

This mindset became very helpful as I started the challenging journey of starting and finishing this book. I have the tendency to start out like a lightning bolt, full of passion and energy, with a sense of urgency and a fire that makes me feel unstoppable. Then as other responsibilities of "life" start piling up I can lose the ability to focus my time and energy on what I feel drives my spirit. I start to run headfirst into obstacles and become impatient and discouraged. If I don't have the time to finish something it doesn't seem worth starting.

This is easy way out. It's easier in the moment to make an excuse or rationalize that it's ok. To think that your dreams are unrealistic or too far out of reach anyway!

Achieving your dreams is simple but not always easy. Someday is today. You need to be committed. Don't give up on your dreams. When other's opinions take my focus away from the task at hand or my dreams, I am not living in the moment.

Realizing this about me and staying committed to moving forward, even if it was a little bit at a time, became increasingly beneficial in accomplishing my goals. Like writing this book, as I type this, I feel connected to my own thoughts and feelings, I'm living in the moment but still aware of the world around me. Instead of worrying about what this book will be to others I am aware of the fulfillment I get in just taking a few moments to write today. It helps me get out of my random thoughts and focus on this moment. It may not make any difference today for how anyone else feels, if I type a paragraph or two, but it makes a world of difference to me and how I feel. Over time, those paragraphs add up and my passion for writing and sharing my journey becomes purposeful in a book that can be shared by all.

Act on your passion, even if it's only a little bit each day, and it will instill in you a sustained inner energy from being present in the magic of the moment.

I was talking with my Godmother and I was telling her about how I was finally writing a book and taking it seriously. I honestly shared with her how I felt and how it's overwhelming because there is so much I want to say and it seems stressful to try and capture the true essence about what I want to share with others; especially when I think about making it good enough for other people to hopefully benefit from reading. I'm so passionate about sharing my journey. It has become a purpose and I want to make sure to capture and give this indescribable energy, spirit and passion justice.

She said just write what and where you're at right now and don't worry about everything else; the other stuff will come out when it's supposed to. How simple, genius and wise, and how vulnerable we are when we open up to someone else about our struggles, but this is where love resides, within our vulnerable selves.

Mark Twain once said, "I've had many troubles in my life, most of which never happened."

We can spend our time being depressed, anxious or worrying about things or we can spend our time doing something about it.

Although some of us think we are great at multitasking in all reality we can only truly do one thing at a time.

All I know is what I know right now. We can always learn or do more but it's ok to be exactly where you are right now. There is a reason for everything and our reality is we are all starting in this present moment.

CHAPTER 9

LISTEN TO YOUR HEART

SHARE YOURSELF WITH OTHERS

Years ago, before writing this book, I decided I wanted to become a speaker at conferences. After the initial excitement an inner resistance and an overwhelming feeling of how to accomplish this goal came over me. I needed a nudge but more importantly I needed to take action. Until I took the first step and started to put together and submit proposals for presenting at conferences, I realized that the reality of me actually doing it was probably zero. As I sat and listened to these great presenters, along with some that I didn't think were that great, I felt the urge to present. I felt like I had the ability, passion and a message to share that would help others.

Unless you take action and do something about your thoughts they are just thoughts.

Over ten years of going to conferences, I kept saying to myself as I sat there in my seat, "I would love doing that...I could do that...I wonder how much he gets paid...I think like that!" I asked someone from the conference committee how much they paid for that speaker and they said, "I think like $3,000 or $4,000", and then I said to myself, "Yeah, I can definitely do that!"

Following your dreams takes courage and commitment. I had to continually nudge myself and put in the extra time it takes to bring thoughts to reality. As we begin adventures into the realm of our dreams, we will constantly be faced with opposition. It takes continued effort. To fill out proposals, start a website, make videos, take the little moments of time where I felt like I wanted to watch Netflix, and instead invest it into becoming a speaker.

It all started with one yes, and then it happened, I was officially a "speaker". The first opportunity sparked the flame. The second one stoked the coals and, at my third speaking gig at a conference, I got a request from an attendee to come and share my experience with their colleagues, and the flame became a full blown fire. The opportunities were always there I just had to go out and get them. By my sixth or seventh speaking appearance, as I received a check for $3,200, I realized that what we focus and act upon really can become reality if we work hard at it. The seed that I planted within my mind years prior at that conference had grown and manifested into my reality.

"Genius is 1% talent and 99% Hard Work" - Albert Einstein

Nothing would have happened if I didn't take that first step, get courageous and become willing. It all happened in the moment, whether I was working on the computer, talking with people before or after my presentation or asking others for help, it all took place in the moment. I started to learn and practice, without worrying about the outcome or what my grandiose expectations were. I just lived and shared my passion, took steps forward and trusted that as long as I had good intentions the results would work out how they were supposed to. I learned as I went, was told "no" plenty of times. (which I turned into a presentation on the "Power of being told No") I started putting together proposals and presentations that now can be submitted and tweaked for conferences and workshops with minimal effort.

Once you have the knowledge it becomes part of who you are. It becomes increasingly easy to do things you once thought were difficult. Each time you face a new challenge and overcome it you get better and it becomes an investment in your purpose and passion. As you grow your purpose you become less and less overwhelmed or worried about the outcome.

An example of the power of "no" started with one of my favorite events I've ever hosted. It was a skateboarding event and competition I called Going Big in the Bay. One of the initial growth opportunities started when I was told "no" when I first presented the idea to my supervisor. I left work that day feeling deflated and on my drive home. I said to myself, "I'm going to just do it because I couldn't understand how an employee who wants to go above and beyond, add to their workload to create something unique and impactful for our community...shouldn't we be at least given the opportunity to try? What was I hired for? If it doesn't work then maybe this isn't the job for me."

There was something I knew deep down, I felt it could be something great, so I started to plan and do it anyway. In less than a month I had a local skateboard shop, professional football players, professional skateboarders, live bands, a radical DJ, photographers, artists, videographers, food, prizes and through the network of the skate-scene, some really passionate support. Someone from "The City" government was finally doing something for them and trying to put effort towards their passion.

I reintroduced the idea to my supervisor after putting this all together. My supervisor asked why I didn't propose this before, she didn't even remember that she told me no! If you follow your soul, have a good plan, take calculated risks and passionately work hard your goal will come to fruition.

The other reason I did it anyway was because it was fun. Even if it had to be on my own time I felt it could be special. I wasn't a skateboarder. In fact I have horrible memories about when I tried as a kid, I think my tailbone still hurts a little.

When you have fun and feel inspired when working on something then work and life takes on new meaning and it doesn't feel like work anymore.

You are uniquely you, so learn and relate to others, but don't try to compare yourself to them. You have something special to give to the world and keeping it to yourself won't help you grow. Growth is essential to the human spirit and without it we lack the ability to become who we are truly meant to be.

It's already been many years since I initially started writing this book, and although I feel more committed than ever, I want to make sure it impacts others. I want to be finished, but when it takes away from and shifts my priority in a way that doesn't reflect and grow my beliefs and values, it is counterproductive for my family and my overall well-being.

These days I notice people, and sometimes myself, engaging with smart phones or social media instead of being present interacting with the people we are with in the moment. In our world today, everyone seems like they are so busy, we don't socialize the same way we used to. Most of us spend the majority of our waking hours at work. When you factor in sleeping, and I'm not even going to get into all the activities we think we have to get our kids to, we might have a couple of hours a day to spend with our family if we are lucky. The last I heard, on average, the amount of quality time per day we get to spend with our family is 37 minutes. So it's good news, and research has shown, that if you spend a short amount of quality time with your kids there is still a positive impact in their overall well-being. Kids don't understand work and all the other reasons you may not be present in their lives, they just want to spend time with you. Sometimes my work-life balance gets a little lopsided and that isn't ok with me. I've been striving to incorporate as much work-life fusion into my life; whenever I can I get my family and kids involved in programs, events, activities and conferences. I also make sure to intentionally schedule time with my family and not save vacation days. I use them for the intent they were given.

I'm not ever going to be perfect but if I continue to practice living in the present moment the best I can and continue to share the best of me that is all I can ask of myself.

If you have something to share, to become a gift, you have to share it, you have to give it away!

CHAPTER 10

FLASH OF GENUIS

Inventing a better me

The universe wants and needs us to be creative to survive but most importantly to thrive. I like to think my inner purpose started as the flash of genius. Like an inventor, the difference between those that thrive and just survive, is acting on that flash of genius. Sometimes it happens suddenly and sometimes it happens over time. We were created to create. A higher genius created trees, rocks, water and all the miracles around us. What we create with the gifts we have been given is what separates us from animals.

A moment like this happened to me when I least expected it. I didn't see it as a flash of genius at the time, in fact, I saw it as the total opposite. The experience started out as a pitfall in my life's journey and ended up being a powerful life changing force. Positive action and time has a way of warping us into a new and better dimension. It was the moment that I began reinvented myself and discovering my true passions and purpose!

Throughout my youth I had tried to be a good boy. I was told that if I was good that people and the world would be good. I've come to realize there is a little bit of bad in the best of us and a little bit of good in the worst of us.

Then the moment came. The moment where all the memories, shame, regrets, thoughts, actions, worry, fear, frustration... built up to the point where the pain was greater than the pain of changing.

MR. JAMES DANIEL ANDERSEN

It happens everywhere, every day. There are flashes of genius all around us.

My problem started many years ago. While growing up, I started to observe the simple addition of drinking alcohol to any event or outing seemed to make the experience happy and jovial. It was something I had grown accustomed to and it seemed to be accepted and celebrated in our culture, or, at least that is how I perceived it. What started out as a really fun way to socialize and build comraderie with friends throughout college and at social events, turned me into someone I didn't want to be and made me act and do things I typically wouldn't do. As I got older, when I drank, it became less and less about the comraderie or celebrations and more about me and how I could change my reality. It actually started to add to my feelings of being overwhelmed or reinforced how unhappy I felt. I didn't learn how to cope with life on life's terms. I always wanted to look and feel like everything was great and didn't understand that the ups and downs of life where just that, life.

The flash of genius changed my life that awful yet magical night...I hit my bottom. I woke up on the couch, everything for the next five minutes seemed remarkably clear. The next 20-30 years flashed before my eyes. In all relative terms, it could be a decent existence, but I wanted to be honest and real and my soul yearned for more. My life was laid out before me and I had a choice on what I wanted, and I knew I had a greater purpose than what I saw in the mirror.

Here I was in my early 30's, beautiful wife, four wonderfully healthy kids, a great job, above average home and yet I felt lost because I didn't seem to know who I was or who I wanted to be. Was this what I wanted my kids to see as a normal set of circumstances that would define their environment growing up? There was an empty and lost feeling in my soul. My purpose, my God, my inner passion knew that I was destined for more than, "this".

In that moment, in my "flash of genius", I made a choice. I didn't know what was going to happen. I didn't know if I would even like the results. But something deep inside me knew that I had to be honest with myself and how I felt and I knew I was meant for more. I was destined and designed to live a blessed, wholesome and innovative life.

I finally saw the silver lining, many years later. It took a daily commitment to dedicate my efforts on working on improving myself. It evolved into a daily practice of continuously learning, failing, growing, trying new things, failing some more, and changing. Throughout these struggles and soul searching I discovered an inner thirst, a quest for always learning and discovering more. I discovered methods and a purpose that works for me and brings me closer to a greater power within myself. There were many positive practices that helped, but the real essence of God's power came to me connecting with other people within the groups of Alcoholics Anonymous. I never would have thought that I would have been guided back to a relationship with God through a group of recovering alcoholics, but that is exactly what happened, and I am so grateful for their overwhelming love today.

Speaking of love, I have an incredible wife, kids, family and friends...and I needed them more than I knew to help me through this period in my life. My life may not always be perfect but it's my authentic life now. By developing my passion and purpose and building a relationship with a power greater than me, whom I call God, it has brought greater levels of love, peace and joy then I knew were possible, even in the toil.

TOIL IN THE SOIL

I once heard a story about a farmer who was nearing the end of his life and was on his death bed. As he lay there, he told his sons their inheritance was buried out in the fields. The riches were in the same soil and earth that has provided for their families livelihood for decades. He gave them the shovels and equipment they needed and told them to go out and plow, turn and toil the soil in order to find it. They went out and turned and toiled up every last bit of dirt and property their father owned and went back to him dirty and tired complaining they had come up empty handed. Their father once again told them they weren't looking hard enough and sent them out again and they worked twice as hard toiling and turning the soil. They went over every last inch of their fields and again turned up empty handed. Feeling frustrated, tired, sore and defeated they trudged back in to see their father, only to find him already passed away.

That was the end of fall, and the sons were feeling resentful and full of self-pity knowing they would never find or get their inheritance now. They couldn't comprehend it and once again went over every last bit of field turning and toiling the earth. They finally surrendered. Winter came and as spring rolled around they reluctantly did the only thing there family knew how to do which was to sow the seeds and plant their fields. Summer flew by and as fall approached they couldn't believe their eyes. The fields which they had worked so hard on trying to find their fathers inheritance had produced a harvest more bountiful and abundant then they ever knew possible. The sons rejoiced together in the riches the fields provided. It took a lot of work, pain and struggles, but in that moment, they realized their father had left them with the wisdom of the toil in the soil for it was in the toil of the earth that proved its worth.

When we realize and look at the toils, pains and struggles of life as a means to mold and shape our character and grow ourselves we have a gift that goes beyond earthly worth.

CHAPTER 11

THE POWER IN PEOPLE

"No significant learning can take place without significant relationships." -James Comer

How can we enter into a pure and intimate relationship if we don't know who we are?

Someone once told me they could tell me exactly who I was by asking the five people closest to me. You become who and what you surround yourself with.

"Birds of a feather flock together".

When I started my road to reinvent myself and fulfill my purpose and passion, I needed to go all in and tried anything. I submerged myself with positive and inspirational books, movies, messages, quotes, music and most importantly surrounded myself with passionate and purpose filled people. When I became willing to be vulnerable, I found that people mostly accepted and loved me for exactly who I was and not who they expected or wanted me to be. At least the people that mattered did. It also made a big difference when I found a mentor and surrendered to my uneasiness and pride of asking for help. People were more willing to help then I realized.

There is no turnkey answer to discovering your true inner purpose. You need to explore and be open to what works for you. Journaling worked for me, but maybe you will discover something else that works for you. We need to continuously learn together. I reflected and wrote down daily what I felt worked and what wasn't bringing me closer to my passions and inner purpose.

It wasn't always easy to discover and accept that, as my life had progressed, I had a lot of acquaintances but not a lot of real friends or sincere relationships. Even more disheartening, was to realize that I had not been a great friend and had lost touch with many people that I once shared moments, memories and a meaningful and loving connections with. Reality started to take shape and as I started to take a step at a time into a new way of living, I began to accept my present circumstances. But I didn't have to believe that this was my future reality.

For me it all started as soon as I surrendered to the fact that I was not living the life that I was meant to live. I realized that I had problems and struggled when my life didn't turn out the way I thought it should. I didn't know what that meant or how it would change the future, but I knew after many failed attempts at trying to mold my outward life to fit my wants and desires, that it was time to mold my inward soul to guide me to my purpose and help interpret the reality of how I see the world.

As the days and years went by, I found that a lot of the relationships that I once thought where past tense were resurrected and became even better than they were in the past. By reaching out and telling people what I was going through and how I felt it connected me on a deeper level with them again.

One of the main reasons we are all on earth, I believe, is to build meaningful relationships with people and help each other become exactly who God put us on this earth to be.

Studies have already documented the link between longevity and social interaction, finding that across time and culture, people with higher levels of social interaction lived longer than those with fewer social contacts. Don't just run out and see how many Facebook friends you may accumulate, I'm talking about real interactions, between two live people face to face. I'm not a big fan of Facebook but if Facebook is utilized for the right intent I believe there is some good that can come of it. If you do utilize it hopefully it leads you to truly connect with one another.

Communities were formed and our human race thrived when people came together for a common good. They then produced churches, community centers, conferences, Facebook and other gathering spaces where people could connect for a common goal.

Connecting with people is the glue that holds our world together. We can all send someone a text or an email, but real connection happens when we take the time to talk to someone.

If we take even five minutes, $1/288^{th}$ of our day, and take time for others it's a sure recipe for a more enriching life. Take time to impact people's lives and the life it will impact the most is yours!

When we are born we don't have a choice in our surroundings and how we interact and interpret the world around us. If we were born into a family that spoke six languages, we too, would grow up speaking fluently in all six languages without much effort. When we are 35 years old and decide to learn something new like a different language or playing the guitar, it seems to take so much effort and commitment. As we grow older we set up barriers for ourselves based on our past experiences making us believe things are not possible. We settle for status quo or get comfortable with just good enough. This is NOT how it has to be.

Building relationships, like discovering our purpose, is not a sprint. It's a marathon with just a bunch of small moments or goals strung together. It takes a step, stride or leap at a time in the pursuit of our true self. Relationships are cyclical, they ebb and flow and take great commitment.

Relationships are a choice. We live in a world that you can now accumulate "friends" on social media or you can swipe through various screens for your next date. How we start and establish relationships has changed significantly. To have a significant relationship we must be our true self and I'm not convinced people show their true self on their "profile".

What I do know is the more we love ourselves the more love we can give to others and find love in return. If we treat others better than we treat ourselves then we will not be able to break through some of the ups and downs that come with a long term relationship. It may take a little longer to find a relationship worth fighting for, but it's worth the wait.

To have a great relationship, whether it's a personal or professional relationship, I believe the sooner you find your passion and purpose the better. The sooner you can recognize and accept who you are and what you believe in the better your relationships will be and the greater depth and impact your relationships will have. People that you have a true friendship and relationship with will love and accept you for exactly who you are, not who they want you to be.

"Life is a course designed to teach us to love." Matthew Kelly

In the past I have been guilty of not loving my true self. I used to struggle being a chameleon. Without even knowing it sometimes, I tried to mold myself to fit in, just to be liked. I'd act, talk or behave a certain way with the intention and expectation that I will be liked or thought of highly. Sometimes my wife would even comment after I spoke with someone and ask, "Why did you talk or act like that?"

It was deep-seeded. In the past, whenever I seemed to open up and "be myself" whether it was in business or a relationship it didn't seem to turn out well. In reality, I was the one who didn't believe in me. I didn't love myself and failed to accept and embrace the real me. I've found the only way to find true joy in our relationships is to find and fully embrace our own unique self.

This is achieved by being the very best real self you can be and loving yourself for the sole purpose you were put on this earth for.

Don't mold yourself for anyone or anything. You are perfect the way you are, with all your faults, warts and far-fetched dreams.

I believe true relationships take place in the moment, so be who you are in that moment and don't worry so much about what people think or feel. The only person we can be is our self and the only feelings we can control are ours.

What is the goal you are trying to achieve? It should bring you joy not misery. I'm not saying it won't be difficult but the simpler your goal is the more focused you can be. Try this with your relationships. Maybe your goal is to be more outgoing or perhaps you need to listen better. All we can do is strive to improve by practicing and like anything you will get better with time.

You have to interpret the steps or the internal goals by listening to your own spirit. When I follow the exact steps as others instead of listening to the spirit of my soul the outcome doesn't seem to work out and I don't feel like I'm on the right path. When I take the time to be still and listen to my spirit and follow the direction it leads me, events in my life turn out exactly how they are supposed to.

CHAPTER 12

SIMPLIFY YOUR LIFE

Simplify your life. One of the greatest attributes of Jesus Christ is he simplified very expansive theories and steps to achieve success. At the place and time Jesus lived there were 613 laws of which the people were to abide by. Jesus boiled down 613 laws and showed how they were all covered by the Ten Commandments. Then he even took it a step further and simplified which two are the most important. Jesus described the two most important as, "Love the lord your God with all your mind, all your heart and all your soul" & "Love your neighbor as yourself". This makes it pretty easy to follow the spirit of the law; we are the ones who complicate it.

We have become addicted to "more" and the normalized chaos in our present society. We also have a lot more social media and lawyers then they did in Jesus's time. Imagine Jesus with a smartphone…ha, no I can't even go there.

We need to recognize that these ancient practices will still work today if we choose to slow down, simplify our life and follow them. If we slow down and start to truly practice listening, learning our thoughts, how we think, how we feel and what our soul tells us is truth we will find peace in all the chaos. We will have the ability to actually see the beauty in the chaos.

There is the answer…easy, right?! Not necessarily, because finding our passion and purpose is pretty simple but that doesn't mean it's easy.

Think about the principles monks have utilized for hundreds

of years. The fact is the principles they've stayed committed to practicing still hold true today, possibly more than ever. As a secular society, we have seemingly conquered the physical nature of ourselves. We have made great discoveries in the mental and emotional field of the brain. But I believe, overall, we have only begun to scratch the surface on experiencing and exploring the great depths and vastness of the spiritual realm.

It may not be easy, but it is simple. All we need to do is discover what works for us. We need to commit to simple practices that can bring us closer to the peace for which we yearn.

Monks wake up at 2 am and practice about four hours of reflection, group and personal meditations before even starting their day. I don't know about you but I don't meditate for four hours to start my day, but I do have a little time in the morning if I make it a priority.

One of the simplest practices people with a clear understanding of what makes them truly fulfilled is they practice gratitude. Start a gratitude list. It's simple; just write down things you are grateful for. Post them around the house or them down next to your bed stand and read and say them when you wake up and before you go to bed.

Hundreds of years ago and continuing today, monks thank God (or divine spirit, creative intelligence, creator...or whatever allows you to focus your thoughts on something greater at work than ourselves) for the water to drink and the air to breathe at the beginning of their day. One of the simplest routines is to be like them and practice being grateful every day. It isn't a new or innovative idea and it's easy to understand. You just need to get in the routine of practicing gratitude every day.

We can take these simple principles begun long ago and implement them into positive results in our modern world.

One of the practices I had to learn, which seems obvious as we do it all day without even thinking, is breathing. I started to concentrate on my breath, becoming aware of how I felt during situations and how it changed my breathing. I practiced feeling my breath and taking time to breath. When is the last time you thought about breathing?

Try it. Right now, take a few moments and focus on your breath. Feel your chest slowly rise and fall. Take notice of the warm or cool subtle breeze that flows through your nostrils. Try to be still and quiet. Draw your attention to your breath. Even if other things are demanding your attention stay focused on your breath. Try thinking of nothing but your breath for a few moments. If you can't stay focused and your mind wanders in and out just accept it, don't label it good or bad, it just is. Every time you try this become aware of how you feel and keep practicing. There was one week where all I did throughout the week was continually practice breathing whenever I remembered and wherever I was at the time.

There are many other avenues to discover what brings you closer to a better you. Some people read books, go to conferences, get counseling or join clubs. There's lots of help out there if you want it. You can pay lots of money to a counselor or even more to go to a 3-day conference to help you find your passion and purpose. I'm not saying these are bad ideas, and they may work for you, but it's absolutely free to just look within you and be honest with where you are at and where you want to be. Seek out people that have what you want and learn from them. Ask them what they do, don't be afraid to ask. If they are truly living a life of purpose they will be more than happy you asked.

When you honestly take a look within yourself and start to become aware of your purpose, some people won't understand. Sometimes the people that are closest to you will be the most confused. When it comes to your passion and purpose, it is intimately yours and meant for no one else.

The moment I wanted to change I became addicted to the quest. I figured I might as well utilize my obsessive personality to better myself and rediscover my passion and purpose. I was willing to learn and became teachable. I was open to new people and experiences.

Think about who you invite to dinner or how you utilize your time. Whatever we surround ourselves with we become. The law of attraction says we will become that in which we submerge ourselves into. I became like a little kid again, a sponge, soaking up anything relevant to my personal growth. I realized the moment I thought I knew everything that I essentially knew nothing.

I talked about writing a book for a long time, but when I finally embraced the action part of the process and committed to this goal, it transformed from something I wanted or dreamed of doing to something I needed to do.

I'd been saying I was going to do it for so long; it was an urge deep within my soul that drove me. I just couldn't ignore it anymore.

I was spending quite a bit of the small amount of free time I had on writing this book and one night my wife asked if my plan was to make money on it. I think that is a natural question and naturally money is something we think of quite often. With this book, it was different. I'm not going to lie, deep down, if I ended up making money I knew it would open up so many more doors to help people. It wasn't the goal though. When you have a deep rooted passion pursuing financial gain isn't the purpose. Think about what you would do if you could do anything, if money didn't matter? If you don't wake up and do something with passion then there is no purpose. Passion drives purpose and writing this guided me closer to mine.

I responded to my wife that I needed to do this for myself. I needed to finish this. Becoming an author and writing a book had been burning inside me for a long time. I couldn't ignore it any longer. I'm not sure I'll ever feel "complete" but if I didn't pursue writing this book past the dream phase, then the reality is I wouldn't be a writer. It's a dream I've had since 1st grade when I wrote, "The Bear That Went to Space". It wouldn't matter to anyone else. I'm living a pretty wholesome life right now. No one else would fault me as I believe any sane person would respect the way I try to live each and every day. But it would matter to me, I would know and I would always wonder, what if? It matters to me and that's what matters. It's like believing in something you cannot see but you know it's real, you can't show it to anyone but it's something that drives your soul from within. I would feel like I didn't fulfill a divine part of me. A gift that God instilled in me that I never tried to nurture and grow.

Have you ever had a dream or urge like that?

Instead of the intent being to make money what if we changed our mindset to...does it bring value to the world? From my experience if your passion brings value to the world the financial side of things will work out!

The road less traveled has always called out to me. If this book and any sentence or portion in it can nudge someone to unleash their purpose and passion in the world and find their true self then that would make it worth the effort. That would make my heart sing. If someone can take away even one thing to help them that is all that matters.

I'm a firm believer, and it has held true in my life, if you fully embrace your purpose and passion then God will take care of the rest. It's like a dream, although it may seem illogical or irrational to others, it's your dream and not meant for anyone else.

Along this journey I realized that there are so many people willing to help. Help comes in many forms. By helping we receive the benefits that shine in the form of kindness, grace and love.

Love then continues to grow and shine even brighter when you open yourself up to being honest and intimate. There is nothing more real and profound than loving yourself enough to be you. Do whatever you can to be the best version of who you are before the world told you who you were supposed to be! Open your eyes to all the miracles.

"There are only two ways to live your life: as though nothing is a miracle, or as though everything is a miracle." Albert Einstein

CHAPTER 13

MIRACLE OR MADNESS

Great news...You get to decide

One beautiful fall day, I awoke to four little people pushing and pulling me out of bed. Good thing I took a few moments to thank God for waking up because the path was already set. First, we made breakfast, cleaned up breakfast, then started cleaning the house, ran to get a part at the hardware store, picked up some groceries, made another meal, cleaned up another meal, ran out and played football with the kids and the dog, then baseball. The dog actually came in handy for retrieving the ball, he was a built in catcher. Then I mowed the grass...you can start to see the theme.

The difference-maker, on whether or not I viewed this day as filled with miracles or madness, was my attitude. Throughout each day I try to see all these "tasks" as opportunities of things I get to do, as miracles. Ok, maybe not the house cleaning, but it does make my wife happy and when she is happy she is a miraculous site. If she is reading this I want her to know she is always a miraculous site, but when she is happy it makes her even more heavenly. These moments become parts of my day that I'm grateful for instead of things I have to do or as chores. If I slow down, stay in the moment, don't get overwhelmed with everything, just focusing on one thing at a time which I have a really hard time doing, I enjoy the moments that truly matter to me.

Don't forget to have fun!

That day I stopped four to five times for some leaf jumping, a leaf confetti celebration and even ate some leaf mud soup made especially for me by my daughter in the playhouse. After showing my son how to trim some bushes, washing some clothes, throwing a roast in the crockpot, showering, cleaning up a mess on the floor and shoveling some food down my throat, I went off to DJ a homecoming dance. This is a glimpse of a random Saturday at our house. When you combine this with trying to find time to talk to my wife, give her a hug or a playful slap on the rear, the only way I honestly can say I make it through the day sane and happy is having a God directed mindset and the power of passion and purpose within my soul.

And on the seventh day, the Lord rested...and I rested on Sunday. How good it felt, to go to church, sit down for the football game, relax and go to bed early on Sunday.

Remember to take time to relax.

We all have to suit up and show up some days, but we need to be aware of when we need to relax and recharge our batteries too. Sometimes we have a lot going on, but don't let life pass you by. If we don't take time to slow ourselves down and enjoy the moments we will miss the miracles. If we don't slow down and connect with others, I mean really get to know them, listen, and take the time to share something beneath the surface we will miss life's most precious gift.

We are like icebergs; most people only show us a small portion of who they are on the surface. The true human experience and the majority of our volume and depth is beneath the surface. Sharing your time with someone, seeing their eyes light up and their heart start on fire for something they are passionate about is an experience you will not want to miss!

My attitude, living in the moment and my passion and purpose make the difference between all these "things" in life being something "I have to do" to something "I get to do."

The same goes for building relationships; it's the little things that make the difference. Spending time with another person, staying in the moment, loving yourself so you can be the true you and letting the cards fall as they must, will make all the difference in the relationships you have with others. Great relationships will help give you the love and power you need to fulfill your purpose and passion.

I was curious how our oldest son would respond when he entered middle school. These middle school years can really make or break some kids as they navigate how they feel about their new environment, classmates and themselves. Friendships become so important and although we can't control everything we try to discuss and talk with him about how important it is to learn how to form healthy relationships.

One of the healthiest relationships we can display in our words and more importantly actions every day, besides our marriage, is our relationship with God.

I always tell people I love them, even my friends and a lot of times people I just met not too long ago. Sometimes I get some weird looks but most of the times if you do it in a very non-creeper way you will at the very least get them thinking. I refuse to quit telling people I love them even if they don't respond as I would like.

I dropped off my son one morning at middle school, as he hopped out the door, as I usually do I said, "Learn a lot, love you, have a great day!" Only this day, I accidently said, "Learn a lot, love you, you guys have a great day!" He turned and said, "you too", and started to close the car door, then he paused, looked back at me and said, "You guys?" I just rolled with it and said, "Yes, of course, you and Jesus", which prompted a nice smirk and a happy shrug, heading off to school for the day with a, "yea, sounds good".

It might have been a slip in wording, but it was no mistake, I believe every little moment happens for a reason. We have to be ready for these moments and when we are living a life full of passion and purpose they seem to happen with greater frequency. God plants seeds in us through these moments. Hopefully these moments grow my son's awareness and a faith that no matter what happens our most important relationship to develop and grow is our relationship with God.

CHAPTER 14

PRESSURE

Don't feel pressured to pick one thing to be passionate about or overwhelm yourself thinking you can only have one purpose.

This can be overwhelming but let's start with how we feel. Does something make you feel like you have purpose, even if it's hard? Then keep doing it no matter how hard it gets, if people say you can't, if they say you're crazy, truly commit yourself even more to the cause. Don't listen to the haters, when you are doing what you love doing people may feel intimidated and jealous. When you become successful at something, naturally, there are people that will try to bring you down.

Always be prepared and on guard, as you will probably have to protect your purpose and passion daily. All it takes is a moment of weakness, letting your guard down to lose your passion. You will run into people that say you can't do it. Thoughts can start coming into your mind about how you're not good enough, or it's too much work and how the easy way out seems like a good choice. The pressures of life can start to build up and we don't find ways to balance ourselves and stay focused and driven to protect our beliefs, we can easily be pulled by negative influences and pleasures that give us immediate relief. These moments happen to us all, but it's what we do next and how we respond in those moments that are a testament of our true character.

If you have any ambition at all of being a leader, you will have to face uncomfortable situations with people. As you are presented with more leadership opportunities and elevate your vision the more pressures you will face.

Leaders have vision, not just a desire to do something great. Desire is personal and benefits you. Vision benefits a much broader scope of people and looks at the whole instead of just a small piece of the puzzle. Being a leader, like building character, doesn't happen overnight. As your passions and purpose start to grow and take shape it will thrust you into positions and places to lead. These situations may feel uncomfortable and raise your blood pressure at first, but don't worry, it's all part of the journey. Learning to overcome and cope with these feelings will be the difference in whether your vision becomes reality or stays as just a desire.

Don't let other people's issues become your issues. Start to become comfortable with the uncomfortable. It's easier said than done, but if you have any drive to be a leader you will be faced with challenges. Putting these practices into action as growth opportunities for self-improvement is the challenge, but every time we face these situations head on we can learn how to control our own thoughts and feelings. Think of these uncomfortable encounters as training grounds for future success.

Remember when you were a kid and learning was so exciting, every little thing was an adventure. Remember that first job when you were a new professional and the "Real World" was at your fingertips. Suddenly you find yourself in a position to make decisions that can create real change. It can be a little overwhelming. My advice is focus on the solutions, connect with each other, learn together, overcome challenges, play with new ideas, laugh at the craziness and help each other through the hard times. When we start sharing our lives and stories...the pressure will seem to fade away.

Staying focused daily towards a goal can be simple. It's kind of a running joke at work, but I'll give you a quick example of something that may sound silly and simple but works wonders for me.

Post-it notes are a simple and practical part of my success. My colleagues joke around about it and they give me flack but post-it's just work for me. I love them. I have inspirational messages, words, steps, visions, processes, mantras and themes all over my desk and throughout books and journals. They have kept me alert, focused and striving towards goals. I need reminders daily to help me move forward through the plateaus and pressures of everyday life.

CHAPTER 15

THE ART OF CHANGING PROBLEMS
into SOLUTIONS

Is there something holding you back from being the best you can be? Then you have to define it and address it.

People often over-complicate and over-analyze problems we face, but solutions start with defining the problem. It's actually simple, what's the problem and are we willing to look at solutions and do what it takes to solve it?

One of the keys to leadership and living in peace is learning how to stay calm during the storm. When you are upset, angry, frustrated, on the surface or deep down, there is really essentially something you can learn about yourself. You do not need to allow the other person, situation or what someone else did control how you respond. Your actions and responses are your responsibility. I have come to discover that there is no problem that a spiritual solution can't solve.

We can accept, change or grow from the experience. We can also try to fix problems. I consider myself a great problem solver, but the problems I'm referring to are sometimes deeply seeded within ourselves. I've come to realize that I cannot "fix" others problems but I can address my own.

We can look at ourselves as the problem or the solution. When we realize all our emotions and thoughts and feelings are our own and we can choose to be different. The way we feel has everything to do with us and nothing to do with anyone else.

As we grow older some people naturally start to become aware that we have the ability to control our own actions and re-actions. If you're anything like me you have to work at developing your ability to be aware and present, calm and true to your-selves and not give others the power to alter your presence and happiness. It is a choice and it takes effort and action to change.

Every day we are influenced and burdened with problems. I can't just live in a bubble but I can make simple choices like; I don't watch the news, unless there is something specific being addressed that is a priority at the time and needs my attention. I do respect the body of work that news and media inform us on, I just feel that it is typically filled with a lot of negativity and problems and not a lot of solutions.

Learn how your emotions and thoughts work within you and learn how to manage and control them, particularly in high stress conversations and situations. Focus on the solution...it will make you better at handling these situations. Treat each day as an arena to learn.

Everyone has colleagues at work or people in our lives that love to complain. When you ask them their ideas on how to make things better or their solutions, they may become upset or de-fensive. If you ask them to lead a task force to make it better, they throw their hands up and say the problems are just too large and have been going on for too long. They seem to be able to tell you all about other people's behaviors, responsibilities or actions but find it difficult to accept accountability for their role in the situation.

We all need to be accountable for our own behavior and actions. What if we added up all the time we waste complaining and gos-siping and spend that amount of time working towards making things better? Can you imagine how much better our world would be? We would easily move the needle towards great on whatever initiative you're working on. It takes a lot of work to change. I believe even one passion and purpose driven person can help change the culture because they will be focusing on solutions not problems.

We are either part of the problem or part of the solution. If we focus on the solution and not the problem it takes the stress and frustration out of the situation.

Marcus Aralias, the great Roman emperor, in 170 AD, became known as one of the great rulers and leaders in history. In his life, he overcame what we may consider to be, insurmountable obstacles. In his role as emperor and his personal life, when there was a perceived hardship, problem or personal anguish to deal with, he chose to think on a higher plane. His constant thoughts were to be the light for his people and himself. He easily could have chosen to sit in the dark but instead chose to live in the light. The one thing that never changed throughout his life was his persistent drive to pursue a greater good. His principles and beliefs made it possible for him to overcome anything.

Living in the light reminds me of my morning runs through the woods near my home, it can be creepy; my eyes can even imagine and see things that aren't even there. The light is rewarding as I pop out into the sunlight at the end of the wooded trail. It makes it so much easier to see clearly in the light. Most of us are looking for a safe path through, a safe place to be great, but there isn't one! Sorry to break it to you, but I don't think finding your purpose is like some get rich quick scheme. It is simple but not easy!

Make decisions and take action for what you feel is right. It can be really hard but also very rewarding. I'm not even sure it gets easier, but as we strive daily to form and shape our principles and beliefs, and continue to practice making decisions that are right for us in the moment, we will grow and so will our purpose. As we continue down our path we will start to intuitively know what to do next. Working on yourself and continuing the pursuit of building your character, establishing your own ideals and principles and being able to confidently address situations with conviction will change your life. Not just for today but for many generations to come.

Believe anything is possible.

As a kid I was instilled with the notion and belief that anything is possible. These days, I do know that although anything is possible, it doesn't necessarily mean it is right, possible or needed for me at this moment in my life or this moment in time.

I realize that there are some things I more than likely won't be;

King of Persia, a Cowboy in the 19th century or a Pirate in the 1500's. I can't invent the flying machine, again, well, maybe not the same. I can, however, learn to understand who I am and become happy with who I am at this very moment in my life. We can reinvent ourselves at anytime. It became my ultimate goal to build a better me. I found peace and joy when I felt like I was exactly where and who I was supposed to be in the moment.

Can we become a person who can look at every situation as an opportunity for growth, regardless of how others define it? Can we look at problems as stepping stones to opportunities for a better life? Is anything possible? Can we learn to accept or change situations in our life and become our best selves? Can we discover our passion and purpose and live the life we've always felt we have wanted to live?

The answer to all these questions and more is **YES**.

If you don't feel like your current situation is bringing you closer to your purpose, then it is time to dig in and discover the overwhelming joy of being exactly who you are in this moment.

Leo Buscaglia wrote, "The easiest thing in the world to be is what you are, what you feel. The hardest thing to be is what other people want you to be, but that's the scene we are living

in. Are you really you or are you what people have told who you are? And are you really interested in really knowing who you are because if you are, it is the happiest trip of your life."

CHAPTER 16

PERSERVERANCE

Have you lost a job, gone bankrupt, faced divorce or have you or someone close to you fallen ill?

When building the structure of our lives, like any builder trying to erect a structure that can withstand the test of time and the elements, it takes time and needs to have a good blueprint. And it needs to be built on a firm and solid foundation.

I am lucky to have five kids to read books to at night. I get the opportunity to be reminded often of these simple yet profound lessons from children's books like, "The 3 Little Pigs" or "The Tortoise and The Hare" which continue to hold true in our adult life. They teach us that if we put in the hard work to build something that will last it will be worth it in the long run.

Throughout our life we will face constant change and if we want to grow we will need to build on a firm foundation that will need to be reinforced from time to time. If we build a solid foundation we will have a much easier time maximizing our purpose. A firm foundation will give us the structure we need to persevere and last the test of time!

Believe in yourself. You can reinvent yourself over and over again. Each chapter in our lives happens for a reason, in the right season. We might not think what takes place in our life is right, what we expect or what we believe is good for us at the time, but we are not in control of the timing. The timing and overall outcome comes from a power greater than ourselves. Be patient and keep moving forward, even if it's only a little each day. Inches add up to miles, but they won't add up to anything if we don't take that first step. Incremental progress is the key to growth. Progress defines our growth and our transformation will start to take shape only through perseverance.

At work, if we lack the motivation or the skill to continue then we need to change and grow. I know I don't, but if you prefer you can let your supervisor change the situation for you. This seems to be the opposite of empowerment, but if we don't move forward and show initiative, progress and ambition, then other people will force this on us and they will do it the best way they know how. Like our parents, although we may not see it at the time, they will do the best they knew how at that time...they are human too.

"We may not like it, but I'm a warrior not a whiner." – Joel Osteen

We can all learn and grow into the best employees, parents, spouses and friends we know how to be. Our other choice is we can continue to be stuck in the past and deal with the same memories and feelings which drag us down or most disturbing of all, we drag others down with us.

One day, it dawned on me how much wisdom is in the book, "The Tortoise and The Hare". In my life, when I started making plans, setting goals and taking manageable risks, a little bit at a time...things seems to work out in the long run.

To better myself, I started to focus on improving my process and my delivery. I also started to try and learn, relate, understand and accept other people for whom they were instead of who I thought or wanted them to be...and realized they didn't have think like I do, and that's ok. I learned not to share certain thoughts or ideas right away but meditate on them for a while or ask people close to me if it a good idea or not. I found people didn't necessarily give me answers but in the confiding of others comes wisdom into yourself and your own thoughts. I had to slow down.

Invest in you; take time for yourself and your true thoughts, even 5 minutes (1/288th of your day), to be quiet and still, away from the busyness of the world. You will start to see a much different world.

We need to persevere and not procrastinate or rationalize why we are not moving forward. If you lack motivation, start identifying what gets you motivated. When you have a good day revisit what made it good. Write it down, then repeat, tweak and try doing more of that. If you lack the skill or method, learn it or find someone else who does it well and learn from them. Personal growth takes time, action and perseverance.

Yard by Yard is hard. Inch by Inch is a cinch. The transformation never ends. I've heard someone else describe life as, "The Beautiful Struggle". Each and every day is a gift and we can treat it as a blessing or a curse. It is your choice. The journey is the prize.

Moving forward steadily but surely, whether it is in your career or your personal life, discovering your personal blend of patience and perseverance will lead to beautiful results.

I heard this story on the radio on the way home from work one day. There was a man, who was not happy with his marriage, and out of desperation he asked his wife sincerely one morning, "What can I do for you today?" After the initial sarcastic rebuff, she picked one thing and coldly said he could do_____. This went on each day and it was quite a rocky process at the start. But he kept asking, "What's one more thing I can do?" Although he didn't really want to this everyday he wanted his marriage to be better. After quite a while he noticed something was changing, he was still asking her, but she was starting to also ask what she could do for him. It wasn't a perfect marriage but it grew a lot stronger and there was a new love forming, a love that wasn't seeking something in return.

There are countless stories on perseverance, I believe as humans we were built with an inner foundation to persevere. We were instilled with an inner drive to overcome challenges and make this world a better place then we found it. We are the ones that have to choose to listen to that inner voice and act on that inner voice or ignore it.

I was at church one Sunday and heard a story about Dr. Glenn Cunningham. When he was only seven years old, a wood stove at his school exploded and burnt his legs. His brother died in the explosion and he was told he would more than likely never walk again. As he lay there in sheer misery unable to speak and barely conscious due to all the pain, he heard the doctor say to his parents that he was not going to make it. He heard it, but in that moment something inside him spoke to him. He made a choice in that moment that he was going to walk again, and do great things someday. Some people die or something inside them dies at the moment someone says they are not going to make it or it's not possible. Others rise up and tell themselves that they are going to make it no matter what. I don't know what the difference is but I can tell you we all have the ability to rise up and overcome anything if we have perseverance.

After many days in the hospital he transitioned to a wheelchair. Then he started walking along the picket fence one picket at a time. To make a long story short, Dr. Glenn Cunningham ended up running a record breaking mile at Madison Square Garden, went to the Olympics and his story became a story of inspiration and testament of perseverance.

His inspirational story didn't end there. The most impressive and inspirational part of Dr. Cunningham's life to me was that his wife and him went on to live on a ranch raising their twelve children and helping youth.

Dr. Cunningham was quoted before he passed away saying

"We have worked eighteen hours a day, seven days a week, to rehabilitate 9,000 wayward or orphaned youths who passed through our care."

We all can have our own stories that are profound and impactful, some of our dreams are just waiting patiently to be discovered and acted upon. Our profound impact will grow when we focus on improving ourselves, the way we talk, our actions and how we treat others. When we improve ourselves the people and the world around us will improve. It starts with one person at a time and that person can be you. The point is you can persevere through anything you set your mind to. As you persevere and progress through your life, your purpose will continually become clearer.

CHAPTER 17

PROGRESS

Definition: PROGRESS: Noun - forward or onward movement toward a destination. When used as a Verb - move forward or onward in space or time.

Progress fuels our passion and whether or not we make the right decision at the time or not, the key is making a decision. Not making a decision is a decision to not make a decision.

Colleagues that I trust and know me are aware that I'm a believer of changing things and sometimes that means making decisions and asking for forgiveness later.

At any given time in our current society, at least half of the people you run into are probably going to disagree with you. They may also get defensive or combative because it causes them to think about changing or takes them out of their comfortable safe zone. If you can't move forward unless you need everyone on board with your vision or choices or want people to like you then you may be stuck in the mud for a long time. I do firmly believe true change takes place within but progress needs to be seen from others for them to buy in to your vision. If this is changing a process or program at work, sometimes you need to take the risk, put the extra effort in, and prove to them it works before people will follow.

I choose to look at failing as a stepping stone to learning. Nothing new would ever happen if we didn't fail. Great organizations see massive amounts of progress and success when they look at failure as an opportunity to learn, grow and make their people, profits and culture better!

One thing I continually work on is listening. I believe many people are like me and struggle with listening. I am making progress but each day is a learning lesson.

I heard a speaker say, to respond better when listening to someone; start by being aware of your breathing and count to three before responding. It felt very awkward and I felt a little dumb at first, as my brain kept thinking about the way I wanted to respond and the three seconds felt like a minute. Instead of thinking of how I would like to interject or react to what the person was saying I practiced waiting until they are done with their thoughts. Each and every time I practiced listening I noticed and became aware that speaking less actually seems to bring on more productive conversations. I also noticed people will say things that helped me connect with them on a much deeper level and produced more authentic relationships. This helped our teams at work become more successful and also helped my personal relationships. It especially helped me in my home life with my kids and in particular my wife.

My father has always been a man of few words. He says what needs to be said, he isn't full of fluff. I had a habit of trying to control the conversation when talking with him. I made an effort to listen and converse with a little more patience and I started to feel like our interactions became much richer and deeper. It had nothing to do with him; it was something I needed to work on. I have developed a deeper understanding and new found respect for my father now.

Listening in the moment and being present will enhance and take our relationships and interactions with people to deeper levels.

I realized when I was growing up I formed some bad habits. I was thinking about what I wanted to say while the other person was still talking, judging what they are saying, figuring out how I was going to respond with my next rebuttal. I realized if

I wanted to truly connect with people I had to make progress in this area. These were things I had to practice while conversing with others. No wonder my Mom always told me I should become a lawyer. Listening without taking over a conversation took lots of practice but it has been enormously beneficial to me and my relationships with others. It also has given me some humility in knowing that I don't know all the answers and others have a lot to offer. It also leaves me with more energy to concentrate on other priorities that need to be addressed because I'm not blowing so much hot air!

You have to forge your own path and reflect on what areas you would like to make progress within yourself. You will make progress on whatever you prioritize and put effort into improving. Strive for perfection but know that progress is all that is necessary. For a life filled with passion and purpose, don't mold yourself for others, but learn and develop habits that are essential for your growth. We are always in the process of change and transformation. When we introduce a daily practice of progressively bettering ourselves we will ultimately make ourselves and the world a better place.

CHAPTER 18

PRACTICE

"Practice what you preach."

"If you talk the talk, you have to walk the walk."

As we progress towards a more positive and profound life, simple age old phrases like these start to take on new meaning.

We practice for many things. Take sports for example, in order to compete and "win" the competition; we need to put in a lot of practice. But when we grow up I feel like sometimes we forget to practice getting better at things like our jobs or our relationships and especially forget to practice finding out whom we really are. We need to be consistently reevaluating and reinventing ourselves to become the best version of ourselves. Being the best version of ourselves is one of the biggest "wins" we can strive for in life.

Our youth look up to professional athletes because of their focus, ability and commitment in following their dreams. What our kids don't always see or want to focus on is all the dedication, practice and effort these athletes put in during those long nights and countless hours of repetition, but that is the part that makes all the difference.

Like working out our bodies to become fit, repetition can also work to make our minds fit. You can change any part of your life, but unless you change your mindset nothing will truly change. Our society is always looking for something on the outside to make us feel better. We are looking for the quick fix when the answer is right in our own minds. We need to continue to practice improving and developing better habits to build our best self. In the practice of bettering ourselves we make others around us better as well.

How do we start? How do we continue to accept change and grow?

Start your morning with thanks. Develop a practice of prayer, meditation, take a walk or drink coffee while reading inspirational messages and stories, write in a journal or write out a gratitude list. Start doing whatever works for you!

Like I said in previous chapters, gratitude lists are awesome. Writing down three things you're grateful for will train and imprint your mind into believing you are grateful, even if you don't feel like it at the moment. Write what you're grateful for on a piece of paper for 30 days and I truly believe you will feel more grateful then you did 30 days prior.

A full and grateful heart exudes happiness and does not leave room for fear or worry.

Keep practicing and further develop what methods work for you.

I tell myself each day how lucky I am just to be alive.

Before I even get out of bed or put my feet on the floor, I thank God for another day. Then I turn and before I even stand up, I pray and connect to something bigger than myself, submitting to Gods guidance and how I can best serve Him and others for just today. I read some inspirational readings that get my mind moving in a positive direction. I practice praying, meditation, and then get in some physical exercise as best I can that day.

When I look at my day as an opportunity to work towards the goal of a better self and motivate myself and others by being positive and having a great attitude, at the end of the day I can honestly say it was the best day I could have had.

This practice didn't start out this simple for me; it came after learning and taking suggestions from others to discover various practices that worked for me.

Try to surround yourself with positive, loving, caring people and read, reflect and learn practices that are positive for you. As you continue to practice you will become better. At some point with continued practice something magical will happen if you are committed. If you are honest, willing and open to transforming your mindset, one day you will start feeling a sense of wholeness and a connection to something greater than yourself. You will feel a sense of belonging and life will take on a new meaning. You will be ready to take on any challenge life throws at you, with love and tolerance.

If I'm presenting a keynote or an endnote speaking engagement on self-improvement, inspiration or finding their passion and purpose, I feel a huge obligation to ensure that participants leave the conference inspired to become a better person. It is up to me to motivate them but it's up to them to take actions and steps to better themselves. It might not click right away, but I guarantee if you continue to practice you will get better at whatever you put your efforts towards.

I'm a big fan in the power of a smile. Simple, right, but scientifically smiling actually tricks our brains into thinking we are happy. I think a smile is contagious and it puts us in a better mood.

Try smiling...I hope you are smiling right now, and I hope you can take a moment to look in the mirror and smile at yourself, give yourself a wink. Tell yourself how lucky you are to be the only you. Then share that smile with others around you throughout your day.

Sometimes when I'm not feeling like my happy-go-lucky joyful self, I simply remember to put on a smile or do something that would make someone else smile. Maybe it's a little note or sticking something they like in their purse or on their desk, grabbing someone a cup of coffee or sincerely asking them how their day is going.

If you are really struggling to smile, find a kid, probably not just any kid off the street as that may be awkward, but someone you know and find some time to spend with them or ask them what they want to do. The answers to our happiness may rest in the minds and hearts of children as they make being happy incredibly simple.

I was in the Army and when I arrived at boot camp one of the first things we learned was to focus on others. We were given a battle buddy and our number one goal was to watch out for their safety and well-being. Think about that for a moment. You're thrown into a new and very challenging environment, away from home with big rigid scary drill sergeants yelling at you and telling you what to do, what to wear, how to act and you're supposed to think about what's best for the guy beside you? YES! If your battle buddy survives this madness now, then there is a good chance he'll survive on a real battlefield. That means if this principle holds true then you will also have a better chance of survival, but you have to fully trust in your battle buddies.

If we are all looking out for each other's best interests and safety then we have a much better chance of survival and success as a whole.

This mentality doesn't only hold true on the battlefield, it is an effective and valuable principle to practice in our everyday lives. No matter what is going on during my day, a simple method to turn my day around is to focus on my "battle buddies." It gets me out of myself, my self-centeredness and focuses my attention on others. Honestly, I think it goes against our natural instincts, but it deeply connects us to others and to our true inner spirit. Getting out of ourselves connects us to the unspoken spirit that connects the world around us because the battlefield we most often engage combat in is within our own mind.

How would we change the world by practicing lovingly asking others how they are doing, without any expectations or how we think they should react? What if we practiced looking out for others best interests without self-seeking? How would it change someone you've been avoiding, because you find them really difficult to be around or work with, by practiced being tolerant and loving with them? Well, it might not necessarily change them but it will change you for the better.

There are the modern day battlefields at work, at home, at church, at the grocery store or driving down the road. These are real world places you can practice being a better you. If reaching out to others doesn't go well the first time don't get down on yourself. Look at it as another practice or lesson in your growth process. There is no end game or expectations anymore, just doing the best you can in the moment. Remember, it's all about progress not perfection.

CHAPTER 19

POSITIVE MOTIVATION AND PERSPECTIVE

Do you focus on the positive or the negative?

Do you know what unleashes your passion more than anything?

Positive self-motivation and your perspective!

I'm starting to think that chances are over the course of the last 10, 100, 1000 years positive people have been the minority. They were probably seen as, a little crazy; they just didn't make a lot of logical sense to the majority of people. When people push through the negativity it makes them stronger and capable of more. Nowadays these positive forward thinkers are seen as some of the greatest and most influential people of all time.

Oprah Winfrey was told she was "not fit for television" and almost every person in the world knows who she is now. She didn't settle for what others said but grew even more passionate and never gave up on her purpose. She learned how to relate and use others skepticism as motivation and found she could use this vulnerability to connect more deeply with people.

Einstein was dyslexic and labeled as mentally retarded. One teacher even told Einstein's father, "He would never amount to anything". Einstein stayed true to who he was and his thoughts and theories and now he is considered one of the most influential people of all time.

Thomas Edison has been said to have famously failed thousands of times. A local newspaper publicly ridiculed him. He spun it positively and just said, "No, I've successfully found out what doesn't work thousands of times!"

What a positive way to look at failure! Its time you start looking at your failures as an opportunity to learn what doesn't work for you.

These people stayed positive and believed in themselves and their purpose and passion. They didn't let other people define them, they defined themselves!

I once heard a speaker say that 85% of people dislike their job. The speaker also went on to say that the large majority of heart attacks happen between 8 am and 9 am on Monday morning. Wake up people! If your job is making you sick then maybe it's time to start rethinking how you want to utilize the time you have left.

Another speaker I listened to once said negativity is costing people around 300 billion dollars a year in the United States alone. Its no wonder that our country is in the midst of crisis. We are making ourselves sick. We then have to treat our sickness to make ourselves feel better, and the cycle goes round and round. We can choose to stop this vicious cycle one person at a time!

It happens every day all over the world, meeting after meeting, interaction after interaction, mostly negative, we've all taken part either activity or passively. All those "problems" we complain about but aren't willing or think we are unable to do anything about them.

It's time to awaken to a better way of living.

Once you make the decision to think and act with a positive mindset, be prepared to protect your positive attitude. You will have people that try to bring you down, call you crazy, might be jealous, and may not understand. It will make them both uncomfortable and accountable so be prepared to protect your new positive mindset.

Your mind and attitude mold you into who you become and shape your life. You may need to change your mindset. You will first need to become aware of your current reality and you have to accept that it's not your job alone. You will need help; my help came in the form of a power greater than myself, which I call God, and surrendering to it. It also came by becoming committed to the journey of learning about me and becoming willing and vulnerable to change. With some people the change doesn't happen because they are resistant to take the first step. If you are willing your life will get better, sometimes quickly sometimes slowly, it's really up to you. I've come to understand that life doesn't really change but how I perceive it makes all the difference.

Perspective is a point of view, perception is what you interpret. Perspective is what you interpret from your five senses: touch, smell, sight, hearing, and taste.

Perception is the process of attaining awareness or understanding of sensory information.

How do you look at situations, do you see the good in yourself and others. Do obstacles and challenges get you excited and turn your "creative mode" on or do you find the negative in everything. If you start looking at life through a different set of lenses your world changes.

It's like when my son got his first pair of glasses; he started to see things he didn't even know existed before. It's time for you to put on your positive mindset and see the world with a different perspective.

"When you change the way you see things the things you see change." Dr. Wayne Dyer

CHAPTER 20

BREAK THE CHAIN

Living a passion and purpose filled life always pays off!

When I was starting my speaking profession, I remember my third opportunity to go and present in Indiana. Leaving early one morning, I drove seven hours, in a snow storm, for a presentation that night. I was fueled with passion and purpose and, caffeine. This opportunity provided no pay. From my experience, as your purpose grows, monetary gains become secondary to sharing your passion. Being willing to put in the effort always pays off. It may not happen right away but the rewards of more abundance will certainly enter your life.

As I put on my Darth Vader costume (I was in drama class for four years in high school and have been known to embrace the stage) and started my presentation. My first thought was, this is either going to be a flop or be awesome. Since I am passionate about the impact the role parks and recreation has in our communities, I was willing to take the risk. Plus, I already drove seven hours in a blizzard for no pay, so I might as well give it my all. Even if I came off a little crazy I could blame it on that!

I spoke with passion and purpose on some of the creative leadership ideas we have implemented as well as our nationally recognized and published health and wellness programs.

After the presentation, I went down to the dinner social and had two gentlemen walk up to me and say, "We know where you get your passion from…Jesus Christ." What a compliment! If I can even be discussed in the same sentence as Jesus then my trip was more than worth it.

On a professional note, taking the opportunity to co-present with the chair of the board of regents for the institute that I spoke at was a good investment. Three years later I was appointed onto the board of regents. From my experience throughout life, being willing always pay off!

I don't want to take myself out of a job or presentation but there are so many simple ways to invest your time that pay off. There are so many good videos about how to find your purpose and passion or work on any aspect of your life. In today's technological age, it's all right at our fingertips. Literally, there are hundreds of YouTube videos on improving positivity, motivation, success, inspiration, physical fitness, relationships, habits, spirituality, academics, attitude and the list goes on and on.

When you become willing to work on this stuff IT WORKS!

There is lots of new research coming out on the study of genes. The good news is research shows you can actually break the chain of negativity!

Genealogy researchers have discovered you can actually deactivate your negative genes. You can choose not to let the past generations of your genealogy affect who you become. Whatever is holding you back from the greatness that you were meant for... that addiction, low self-esteem, abuse, anger...you have the choice to break the chain. I think it all starts by loving yourself enough to change.

This is so exciting! This means we can actually change the future for the better. We can alter how our family tree and how future generations respond and view the world and it all starts with us!

Negative traits can be passed down over four generations.

Ernest Hemingway, one of the most proclaimed authors of our time, committed suicide in 1961. His sister committed suicide five years later, his brother thirteen years later; his father did before him and his grandfather before that. I wonder what his family tree would have looked like if Hemingway would have chosen to break the chain.

You must have a certain level of faith that you can do it. Start to train your mind to know, believe and expect life will work out; you are destined and designed for greatness.

Have you failed 1, 100 or 1000 times?

It doesn't matter how many times we've failed. We can choose to think like Thomas Edison when he said, "I learned what didn't work thousands of times". He grew from the negativity and knew without doubt, that it would work out. He was a chain breaker! He knew he was made for greatness and so are you!

All you have to do is your part. What I put my time, energy and focus on will become who I am.

Don't judge anyone. I heard once that it takes $1/10^{th}$ of a second to judge someone based on appearance.

Take this $1/288^{th}$, or 5 minutes of the day, scenario. What if we give people a break? I'm not telling you to be a doormat but if we looked at a negative interaction from a different perspective. If you find yourself on the other side of a five minute negative experience with someone, maybe it was bad timing. Maybe you caught them in a moment after some bad news or maybe they were dealing with something very grim. We don't know what they have dealt with the other 23 hours and 55 minutes of the day. Give them the benefit of the doubt.

Do we know who they are? Have we asked how we can help? Do we lend a listening ear without judging? Do we practice loving people regardless of how they act? We don't always know what other people are going through? Do we make an effort to be the best husband or wife, dad or mom, brother or sister or friend we can be? Do we practice loving and encouraging people throughout the day, building them up when we have a chance? Do I treat others with the same patience, kindness and gentleness that a few of my mentors and loved ones have shown me?

It's time for us to be chain breakers!

Our world lacks empathy and compassion. As soon as we realize we aren't perfect our lives get much easier. If we were perfect then we would have no useful purpose in this world. If we judge people we are also judging God, as everything in God's world happens for a purpose and a reason. A lady once summed it up pretty straightforward for me when she said, "God don't make no junk!"

If I judge or gossip about anyone I'm really just trying to build myself up to be more important or above them. We are all loved the same and instilled the gift of life from the very same source that has always been and will flow in and through us all until we meet eternity.

We immediately judge people before we ever take the time or effort to know who they really are. Most disturbing is we judge ourselves, which is the cause of most our pain and suffering.

I believe everything happens exactly how it is supposed to. This is not my cosmos to run and thank God for that, I feel I can barely handle what is in front of me sometimes!

It may sound weird, but I have come to think that at some point in our lives we must learn how to become better at life. We must relearn how to hope. We must learn to love, trust again, embrace our own uniqueness and others special talents. We must learn to have empathy and compassion. We must learn to live a life of passion and purpose. We must learn how to be us in this crazy world and live a life full and complete.

I believe you will never find true happiness and fulfillment "out there". It may bring you instant gratification but those feelings are temporary and then you eventually find yourself back in the same place feeling unfulfilled.

Build your life around your principles and run the race for the long run. You may be in a perceived "good" position one day having "power" or "influence" and then the winds of change may come swooping in and you are suddenly exiled or you lose something you thought made you worthy!

Or the reverse cycle may happen where you feel like you're down for the count; you have nothing left to live for. Keep pushing through, good tidings are on the horizon. I read a lot of books and watch a lot of movies and throughout history there are thousands of examples, when a seemingly good or bad situation, in the long run turned out to be the totally opposite! Stay positive and do what is right because it is the right thing to do. Become willing to do what it takes. You can break the chain! Know that it will work out for the better in the long run. Living a life filled with passion and purpose always pays off!

"When you start to become aware of the fact that you manifest what you think, you get pretty serious about what you start to think about." - Wayne Dyer

Successful leaders always think things are going to work out. They always are preparing for a positive experience. Successful people are positive and think about how great each and every opportunity is and how it's going to bring them success. Successful leaders are CHAIN BREAKERS!

When we focus on everything working out for the better, great things will take shape in our minds and thus will also transform our lives!

Today, whenever I go into a situation whether it be at work, speaking in front of hundreds of people or at home with my family. I try to think so passionately that it's all going to work out, it's going to be inspiring and I'm going to bring so much love to this situation that only goodness can be the result!

CHAPTER 21

BE YOU

"Being who you are should be the easiest thing in the world; we make it the most complicated!" -
Leo Buscaglia

I may not have taken these writings from thoughts to book form if I didn't have people that love and support me for exactly who I am. We all need people in our lives that accept and love us for exactly who we are. Growing up my Mom and Dad were incredibly loving and supportive. To a certain extent, it didn't matter to them what I wanted to do or become as long as I was happy. They probably were even a little too accepting at times but it allowed me to discover for myself who I was. Even if you are going through a time in your life that is difficult, the most important person to accept and love is yourself. Never forget to **BE YOU!**

From the time I was young, I felt an inner urge to learn, explore and find my own way. Maybe it was choosing my own adventure books, Indian Jones movies or my vivid imagination, but I knew my path needed to be an adventure as I couldn't see myself fitting into a particular job or category. I feel like school has a tendency to push people into boxes and attempts to tell us we could dream, but we better have a realistic backup plan. Educators preached, go ahead and dream big, but not too big. From my perspective, the education system seemed to function much differently than fostering our soul to believe anything was possible. It functioned more like a conveyer belt on a big machine to keep the country running.

I had a hard time seeing myself having a traditional career. Each time I fought the urge to follow my own path something built up inside me. Over the years, I kept covering my dreams with layers of reason why I didn't have time to pursue my purpose, but the inner urge was always still there.

I'm grateful I was given opportunities to start a good career path and provide a great start to our beautiful family. But I'm more grateful I continued to feel the urge to follow my heart. Like I said, I am grateful, but in hindsight, I'm glad I struggled just enough with the thought of only sharing my passion and purpose within my traditional job. It led me further on my journey to speaking, presenting and writing.

I knew God had created me to do something bigger than myself. I had to get to the point where I needed to do this because it was part of who I was. Knowing and being who you are has to be your number one priority.

Sometimes you have to find out what you don't like doing to be motivated to continue the pursuit of what you do enjoy doing.

The summer between my senior year in high school and my freshman year of college my Dad helped get me a job at the factory he worked at for over 30 years. I knew after one summer that I didn't have the strength he had. It only took me one summer of waking up at 4 am, hopping in a van with a bunch of other factory workers to get to work in time for my 6 am start to realize that no matter what it took I definitely knew I didn't want to do that unless I absolutely had to.

I must have been seriously willing to do pretty much anything else besides work at that factory because I joined the Army the next summer. Ironically, I spent the next summer waking up at 4 am, getting screamed at by drill sergeant's during basic training, but for me it was better than going back to that factory.

It took me a long time to see the unconditional love in my Dads story. My Dad made that personal sacrifice every day to provide a better life for his family. It allowed me to go to college and follow my dreams. Selfless service for others is one of the main ways we can live a purposeful life. My Dad is a true testament of selfless service. He worked the swing shift for over 30 years at that factory to provide a purpose-filled life for his family.

There are many people who have intentionally and sometimes unintentionally showed me how to be me. We can find lessons in everyday life and find our truth if we open our hearts and minds. We also can open our eyes but some of life's lessons aren't meant to be seen right away.

Over the past 17 years, my wife has stuck with me through some tough times, has accepted and loved me for all my craziness. She has always challenged me to utilize my gifts and to be me. I couldn't always grasp her intentions at the time, but over time, I have come to realize the outpouring of love in her heart.

Everyone has someone like this in their lives and if you don't they are not hard to find if you are open. Be open to accept people for who they are, receive help and support. Be willing enough to keep pushing forward when the going gets tough.

I am blessed to have people in my life like my wife, mom and godmother. My godmother, bless her heart, said, "I was like a little drop of dew from Heaven when I was born."

Then she literally went on to say that I fought and cried all the time, came out fighting and I still am fighting today! I continue to fight for what my beliefs are and for people. I hope to help others find their purpose and passion. I hope to inspire myself and others until I die and go to that perfect heaven.

WE NEED TO FIND OUR SWEET SPOT.

Now my days are filled with learning, building my best self, trying to help others, surrounding myself with good passionate people and hopefully making a difference in the world. My hope is everyone can realize their passion. You can do anything. You can accomplish whatever you put your mind and soul into. Your reason for being is that sweet spot between what you love to do, what you're good at, what you can make a living doing and what the world needs. If you're not able to figure out the answers to all these questions start to get out there and learn, build relationships, ask for help, figure out what processes and patterns work for you. The sweet spot may not be apparent all the time, but similar to life and your passion and purpose, the journey is not a straight line. It's filled with a beautiful array of ups and downs, rainbows and storms and if we can be courageous enough to love ourselves and accept others for who they are, we will get the opportunity to have deep and truly meaningful relationships throughout our life.

If you haven't already, take the next couple minutes and grab your journal, a notepad or a post-it or just write it down somewhere in this book. Before you write what inspires you, think about what, where and who you want to be. It doesn't matter what stirs your inner passion and purpose. Whether it's personal, professional, spiritual, physical, write it down. Even ONE thing you're going to work on, I'M SERIOUS, write it down. Jot it in your notepad or I-Phone, somewhere you are going to see it often, with the today's date and then post it somewhere where you will see it often.

Be humble enough and always remain teachable. The greatest teachers and successful people in the world have mentors, read lots of books and are open to learning at any age. They accomplish their goals by writing them down and visualizing them. What you can imagine in your mind can become your reality. It needs to motivate you to move forward and keep believing. Don't listen to the critics. If you feel the passion and if it helps you draw closer to discovering your purpose, DO IT!

I was listening to a speaker at a conference who had experience spending time working with end of life patients and his story make me think. He said, of the people he cared for, at the end of their life, one of the biggest regrets is they didn't feel they lived the life they were meant to live. They felt like they were living the life that someone else wanted them to live or they didn't do the things they were truly passionate about.

BE YOU!

No one dies alive!

If you could do anything, what would you want to do 7 days a week?!

Now, where do you see yourself, what will you be doing, what do you want to be doing in 1, 2, 10 years, 20 years...?

I am passionate about_____ (insert whatever you want to do or be) today! If you start today, one step at a time, over the course of the 30 days, a year or 2, or 10 years, can you imagine what's possible?!

It's essential to have long range goals and a vision for where you see yourself in the future. Just remember, it happens and is shaped one day at a time, in the moment.

Someday is today!

I hope to meet you someday. Maybe see you at some conference or workshop. My hope is you can walk up to me and say, "Hey, I started that business...", "I got that promotion...", "I quit that job and stayed home with my kids and started selling herbs at the farmers market..." Whatever it is I know I will feel the passion in your words and the energy in your soul.

Better yet, you tell me you are living life and being you! It's the real you and you're happy and fulfilled. You love yourself for exactly who God made you to be. You can sit quietly and be at peace, joyful about your journey because you are giving it your all.

I hope you find as many blessings in your journey as I've dis-covered thus far. I know there are many more to come as we con-tinue to grow our passion and purpose.

CHAPTER 22

PRAYER

There will be times in our life's journey when we feel like we don't know which way to turn. We may feel at a standstill and our passions and purpose may feel stagnant. Try to become awakened to recognize this point as just another great opportunity for growth.

**"Don't worry about anything, instead pray about everything"
Philippians 4:6**

Sometimes you may feel there is nothing else you can do. You may get the point where you must surrender to what is. It may not feel like it, but that is a perfect time to put your energy and time into developing yourself. I have never met or heard of anyone who has stayed truly committed to taking the time to develop themselves, come back later, and say it wasn't worth it or their life wasn't any better.

When I was a young boy I remember being instilled with the practice and blessings of prayer before I went to sleep at night. I still say the same prayers today with my own children that my mom and dad said with me many decades ago. "Now I lay me down to sleep", "Jesus thank you for another day" and "God bless others" are 3 sets of prayers that take about 5 minutes, or $1/288^{th}$ of our day. Choose whatever prayers or sayings you feel work for you. It is a great way to end the day, quiet our minds and thank God for another blessed day.

I was blessed to have my mom stay home with me when I was young. When she did go back to work I would ride with my mom on her way to work and she would drop me off at my grandma's house. My mom tried to put me into a home day-care once. Apparently, I wasn't meant to be with others for that segment of my life and fought staying there like the plague. I threw a fit pretty much daily, until my mom brought me to my grandma's to take care of me. What little boy wouldn't want to stay with his kind-hearted grandmother instead of at a house with a bunch of kids he doesn't know?

My grandma lived in a majestic slice of heaven. Beautiful rolling hills in the country on an old farm with hundreds of acres to explore and frolic, a stream to fish, barns to explore, cousins to play with, animals and nature to observe.

On the 15-20 minute car ride down to my grandma's my mom would say prayers and I would listen and eventually started to say them with her. I chose to sit in the back of the minivan as it was like my own little quiet place. I didn't know at the time how these practices and the power of prayer would come full circle back into my life many years later.

I was good at memorizing and reciting the prayers. One day my grandma even asked her priest to meet and listen to me. They just sat there as I recited verbatim almost all of the main prayers the Catholic church had people learn.

This was a great foundation but as I repeated these prayers, as I grew older, I didn't feel I interpreted, felt or understood what the prayers meant to me at that time. When I went off to college I think I got further away from those simple prayers and lived more vicariously. I didn't take the time to be disciplined or stay connected. The social agendas in college didn't seem to flow and align with my religious upbringing.

We sometimes have periods in our life that we feel we want to live in the darkness and not the light. The darkness allows us to hide. The light is bright and truthful. I wanted to keep hiding how I felt but the light is persistent. It kept pulling ever so slightly at my soul even in my darkest moments. Ever since I was young I knew there was something greater that bound us together. The light was always there, it just took my eyes and heart a little while to find and readjust to the brightness. But once the door is cracked open we can't help but continue to open up to the light.

I'm glad our spirituality takes on a journey of its own within us otherwise it would not be our own discovery. Who really wants to be told how to do something, especially something so deep and personal? I was blessed to journey back into the benefits of a practice of prayer. To me prayer is a great way to continually find myself and comprehend God's plan for me. It's also a great practice to bring us as close to God and to our true self as we can be each day. I treat prayer more as a bridge to conversing with God then just reciting prayers today.

Don't take my word for it. If you are at a point where you don't know what to do, nothing else works or you feel an urge to rediscover or enhance your prayer or spiritual journey, try it out for yourself. There are so many different sayings, slogans, messages and prayers to choose from. Find what works for you. My only plead is that you give the best effort you can at the time, make it consistent and don't give up.

The biggest transformation that occurred in me is when I made a habit out of praying every morning and every evening. Then I decided to take it a step further. Throughout my day I discovered prayers, positive affirmations, readings, music and videos that helped form a conscious contact with God. The practice of prayer, slowly over time, was the basis to reforming a rich and meaningful relationship with God.

Now some of my prayers are memorized but have also developed into more of a conversation. I can have various levels of conversation with God and feel a conscious contact with Him throughout my day. I find peace and direction as He helps guide me, forgives me, protects me, challenges me and understands I'm not perfect.

The power of prayer is like watching your own kid grow, you don't recognize the change on a daily basis because you're so close to it. Then relatives come and visit, who haven't seen them for a few months, and are amazed how much they grew.

I'm kind of a numbers guy. I went to a conference one time where one of the speakers said we touched our phones up to 2641 times per day. Wow, imagine if we touched base with God 2641 times a day! From my experience, building a relationship with the God of your understanding is essential for spiritual growth. Without it our souls are restless until they find rest in God. The closer I can stay to God throughout my day the better my day goes.

PUT GOD FIRST IN THE MORNING.

I put God first in the morning. Talking to God before talking to anyone else is important because my day becomes God directed instead of James directed. Trust me, whenever I have James be the director of my life things can easily get messed up.

Prayers can be as simple as the lessons you learned as a child. My mom and grandma taught me when I was young to say, "Please" and "Thank you". We may not realize it but something as simple as manners are like little prayers that make a big difference.

In the morning, I make sure to thank God for another day. I ask him to please guide me followed by anything you need help with. Whatever works for you to direct your thinking. "God, let me live in your light, please direct my thoughts and actions so I can serve God and others the best I possibly can today...Thy will be done." Then at night, I say thank you for the blessings throughout the day and showing me what I need to continue to work on, before going to sleep.

These are honestly just examples off the top of my head. There are so many great prayers that I utilize and as I find or rediscover new ones I love trying those too. The St. Francis Prayer, The 3rd step prayer, Our Father and the list goes on. Those are just the tip of the iceberg of what prayers and mantras have helped me throughout the years. As part of our spiritual growth, the power of prayer holds no bounds, nor depth, height or width. It can be a journey we explore and benefit from for the rest of our lives.

Purposeful prayer with intent can change the world. When you pray, ask God with your heart what you need help with. Keep praying, not only when you're struggling but also when life's miracles are celebrated. Always pray for others and not for selfish wants. Pray for yourself only if it is meant to help others. Whatever you ask for in prayer will be answered, it just might be Gods will and not what you thought you wanted or needed. We cannot comprehend the reasons why things happen the way they do sometimes.

"Therefore I tell you, whatever you ask for in prayer, believe that you have received it, and it will be yours." Mark 11:24
"If you believe, you will receive whatever you ask for in prayer." Matthew 21:22
When trying to figure out my next step, once I hear the answer or direction, the challenge for me is taking action. It takes continued commitment and having faith even when the odds seem insurmountable.

When you start praying and asking God for His will instead of what you want, the power of prayer will start to shape your life for a greater purpose.

This is not a one-time deal. There was a large period in my life when I was really just going through the motions. I only concentrated and prayed when the purpose was to get something or to get out of a tough situation. My prayers sounded more like requests or blackmail. You do this for me God and I promise I'll shape up. You give me this God or get me out of this jam and I promise I won't do it again.

Now, after years of fighting and trying to do things my way, I pray with so much more faith and patience. The answers will come in God's perfect time, not when we want it.

When we start to feel better and things seem to be going our way that does not mean now we can stop praying. If you work a daily practice of prayer into your life, God will do the rest. There are days for me when it seems like the connection is weak and it seems like I'm running through the motions. It's ok, God is always there, even when you can't seem to invite him into your life, he is waiting patiently and with precision for when you are ready. God isn't running through the motions, he has plans for you that are undeniably divine. God made you to be exactly like you are. You are not random, if you needed to be different you would be.

The shortest and most impactful prayer for me is, "Thy Will Be Done."

You can also add this simple four word prayer to any request or prayer that you come up with.

Simple sayings that are easy to remember like this four word prayer or acronyms like the ones below written or posted where you will see them often can help too.

G.O.D., which stands for **G**ood **O**rderly **D**irection.

E.G.O., which stands for **E**dging **G**od **O**ut.

At some point it comes down to a matter of faith. If you add positive logical practices to better yourself, inevitably life will get better, but something still may be missing. Only God can fill that void. There is no room for fear where faith resides. If you surrender and submit yourself to the God of your understanding and serve Him your faith can move mountains. Choosing to believe in God or not to believe in God is a choice and comes down to a matter of faith.

Depending on which side you're on, God or evolution, the debater can back up their choice with evidence which seems to back up their claims. But for me there is an unexplainable gap in evolution, something still had to come from nothing.

There are miracles and experiences in my life along with a feeling that I cannot describe when I try to explain what having God in my life means. I can't give it justice. Trying to explain and comprehend the overwhelming magnitude of creation and God is not humanly possible. At some point it comes down to faith. But like I said, either way God or evolution it comes down to a matter of choosing to have faith. There are plenty of books, movies and experts out there and I found that the facts also point towards an answer, and the answer is God. Find out for yourself if you question your beliefs, don't take anyone's word for it, you are not just dealing with life and death but eternity, and that's a very long time.

I try not to look or perceive things as good or bad. I cannot tell the future and the past has already taken place, I cannot change it, but I can change myself and how I think about it!

Shakespeare said, "There is not good or bad until we think."

Spirituality, like the sculptor, we shape our character and principles over time. It takes patience and dedication.

When I first started my spiritual journey, I found that there are more people that practice growing their spirituality than I thought. They just don't broadcast it like cooperate America does, but maybe we should. It was hard at first to start getting into what spirituality meant for me.

I became honest, open and willing to ask people and research various methods and teachings.

H.O.W., another acronym which stands for being **H**onest, **O**pen and **W**illing.

One thing I found common throughout all the worlds various spiritual practices is they focus on the inner self being fulfilled and awakened.

"The kingdom of God does not come with observation; nor will they say, 'See here!' or 'See there!' For indeed, *the kingdom of God is within you*". (Luke 17:20-21)

The transformation happens in the hearts and minds of people.

We have had exponential and dramatic advances in the growth of knowledge; technological achievements, medical marvels and everywhere you look you are witnessing breakthroughs for something or another. We are now in an age where the spiritual and universal truth is becoming main-stream. People were once looking for answers "out there" and now are realizing the power of their own mind.

Adventurers of the mind and our neurons continue to find incredible links to the science and the ability our own minds have in discovering new pathways, unlimited and untapped potential and possibilities just waiting to be discovered. We've explored almost all ends of the earth and now we are exploring the universe around us. We are even trying to send rockets to Mars and may inhabit another planet someday soon.

There are no depths or heights to the power of the mind and the love of our souls. It's crazy to think there is probably as much unknown about the vastness and unfathomable abilities of the brain as there is about the universe. Our brains are essentially universes. We are all universes within and endless universe. When you factor in the awe that we and everything around us came from the same source, then we are all part of each other and one in the same. The power of this source is within each and every one of us. We can explore our inner passion and purpose our whole lives if we choose. When we make a personal choice to change the world and how we see it we change the world. Yes, we can change the world by just changing ourselves.

If you want to try and practice looking at life or the world through a different lens just look to children.
We think our daughter has a strong spiritual connection because she is very in tune with the spiritual world. She has had occurrences where she has described, in vivid detail, the visits of a deceased Uncle, Father Jerry, who passed away after 50 years in the priesthood, on Christmas night.

We had to rush our daughter to the hospital . Many days after she came home she described, out of the blue, as she was hooked up to all these machines, Father Jerry being in the room with her holding her hand. He came down and kissed her, letting her know it would be ok. Little did we know how serious her condition was, as she lay in the hospital, until the doctor told us afterwards.

If you need more proof of perfect placement, look to nature. Things just are as they are supposed to be. There had just been a hurricane which came through where I was speaking at a conference not too long ago. Amidst all the fear and loss I heard something on the radio about palm trees. Palm trees are perfectly designed to withstand hurricane winds, their segmented trunks, even up to how the branches are formed and the roots are started.

That's why there are no oak trees on the beach.

The natural world is designed in a particular and miraculous way. There is intelligent design all around us, we don't always have the ability to comprehend or understand it and we can try to be scientific, but there's always a gap and that is where faith comes in. We have to decide whether we believe or not, either way it's an act of faith.

Deep down within us we are born with a fundamental feeling

that there is something greater than us at work.

SOUL, SOIL, SOLE SEARCHING

One morning while on a walk, which at that time I started making part of my morning routine, I stopped by a freshly plowed field. I took a few moments to take in the patterns and design of the soil, I slowly crouched down, took my bare hand and scooped up a fresh handful of cold wet dirt. I started thinking, repeating…*SOUL, SOIL,* and SOLE…and as I alternated hands as I packed that cool clump of dirt in my hands, I felt in that moment how everything in life was interconnected. I thought about how a part of this clump of cool soil could have traveled over the years from afar, the distant lands it has seen and how old it might be. In that moment, I felt connected to every little grain of soil and knew I wanted to live life as full and with as much love and passion as I possibly could. I wondered if someday someone like me would pick up a clump of dirt that contained a little piece of my soul thus connecting me to them. Who was I holding? Were they allowing me to be able to see the answers into a new realm of the cosmos? Did they help me unlock a vast wisdom that we are essentially just all one in the same, connected together so meticulously by a universal power greater than ourselves?

This moment wasn't planned or expected, it just happened. That is how life is, it just happens, and it's up to us each and every day to grab and hold on tight and enjoy the epic journey it has in store for us.

When I started my stroll back home, I was thinking about what else this moment might mean for me. I thought about starting a business called Soul, Soil and Sole with the mission on self-improvement (soul), giving and getting back from the earth (soil) and finding your sole purpose in your life (sole). Thus SOUL, SOIL, SOLE was started. Some of my best ideas take place in the joy and unexpected magic of the living in the moment.

This became a starting point for a philosophy I'm attempting to build upon every day. Live life each and every day with passion, purpose...and enjoy the epic journey! I don't even really know for sure what it is all the time, but I'm just acting upon it and taking the next step, one day at a time.

FAITH WITHOUT WORKS IS DEAD

The only difference between me and someone who wants to do something is I'm doing it! I used to be a lot of words and no action. Then I started to understand what people meant both personally and professionally when they said, "actions speak louder than words", "practice what you preach", "you create your universe" and "you choose your own destiny".

Our minds are so powerful that if I understand my inner purpose and how my mind works ANYTHING I put my mind and focus on can come true if I work towards it.

Now, you have to be ready to accept the results of the choices you make, and you also have to realize that not making a choice to do something is also a choice. In my life I'm fortunate to realize that no one or nothing can actually make me truly happy, at peace and fulfilled. I had to learn and realize that the journey was the gift.

There are many mysteries of the world. Routinely praying can be a game-changer. If we do our part and believe then God can accelerate our lives. You may not know where to start.

A simple prayer in times of reflection I've said over and over is the *Serenity Prayer.*

God, Grant me the serenity to accept the things I cannot change, The Courage to Change the things I can and The Wisdom to know the difference.

It may take time and you may need to explore what works for you but if you start to introduce the habit of talking, becoming open and willingly allowing the God of your understanding into your life, your life will grow in ways you never anticipated.

I accepted that I don't have the skills or the knowledge to even come close to understanding why some things happen. That is why the simple prayer that has worked wonders for me over the years is, **"Thy will be done".**

I've said these types of simple prayers over and over and over again in times of confusion, frustration, worry, fear, anger and struggle. At times it didn't seem to be working but if you make it a daily practice throughout your day at some point there will be a moment where you realize that something has changed.

There are some good habits and bad habits. I don't like that I have a habit of eating an entire row of Oreo cookies every time I open a package, but I have no problem admitting that I have formed a good habit of prayer.

Now, I say these types of prayers not only when I am struggling, but every day to thank God and accept His will and when I practice these things daily my life feels connected, full and abundant. I feel grateful for the gift of life.

CHAPTER 23

PATIENCE

Be patient, remember, you can't pull a plant to grow faster, you will kill it! You have to just nurture it and patiently watch the beauty awake in its own time.

The Bamboo Tree

This reminds me of bamboo trees and how they grow. The seed sits patiently in the fertile soil for years, hardly growing upward at all for almost 5 years.

What we don't see is what is happening under the ground. The bamboo seed is sprouting and expanding its roots outward and downward deep, strong and securely building a solid foundation. Then when it's ready and the time is right the bamboo tree, in a matter of week's shoots up to over 60 feet tall.

We don't know when our time of abundance and growth will take place but if we stay committed and have faith it will happen. Everything takes place when it is supposed to.

WE CAN START OVER EVERY DAY

The Lotus Flower

In order to grow, the beautiful lotus flower starts out as a seed which needs to be covered in moist, wet muck and mud and left in the dark. Just as sometimes a person needs to go through a dark time in their lives to grow into their true selves and find their purpose.

The Lotus flower becomes a beautiful flower during the day

then retracts at night and then starts opening in the morning into a full bloom in the afternoon and the cycle repeats itself daily. Buddhists sees the flower as a symbol of rebirth, each and every moment we are born again.

EMBRACE YOUR UNIQUENESS

To me there is no such thing as better, just different; it's just how we interpret it. We might not be able to comprehend it in this moment but everything is perfectly the way it is supposed to be. Each and everything is meant for a particular purpose. There are so many memories we are holding on to and all we have to do is let go and forgive. We are uniquely special and made for a particular purpose. There is no single person out of the almost 8 billion people on earth that is exactly like you!

Divine providence is always at work and beyond my human understanding.

Purpose and Passion is within each one of you and it's up to you to really know and truly get to the root of who you are. Be radical, which means the root of things, the truth, and embrace and enjoy the process of continuing to learn and grow each and every day to find that peace we all seek and to become our truest selves.

We will be tested, the closer we get to the truth the more the world will test our commitment to it. At one time or another we will be faced with skeptics and people who will try to test our beliefs. We may not feel adequate to answer or defend the truth but fear not, truth cannot be diminished.

"The Truth is like a lion; you don't have to defend it. Set it free. Let it loose; it will defend itself." - St. Augustine

So if truth sets you free and love endures all things then you will not have to worry about anything. Once you find it give it all away, then go get more! Giving of ourselves to others and loving one another with no expectations of what we get in return will give us more than we ever knew was possible. One of the most profound goals to strive toward is unconditional love.

"...wisdom lies in the realizing that love is the only way. And yet, even once we realize this, it can be a daily struggle to apply its wisdom to the events of our lives. It is not our natural inclination to love unconditionally, especially when we have been wronged." - Matthew Kelly

Agape Love is unconditional love. "God is Love." 1 John 4:8

"Our yearning for to be loved is a yearning for God." Matthew Kelly

We are meant to be loved and to love one another. I'm big into love because I believe God is Love. Each night before my daughter goes to bed before I leave her to dream, we have a tradition of saying, "Faith, Hope & Love...and the Greatest of all is Love." It comes from the passage in the Bible that was read at my wedding, The Way of Love.

Corinthians 1:13.

"If I speak in the tongues of men or of angels, but do not have love, I am a resounding gong or a clanging cymbal. If I have the gift of prophecy and can fathom all mysteries and all knowledge, and if we have a faith that can move mountains, but do not have love, I am nothing. If I give away all I possess to the poor and give over my body to hardship that I may boast, but do not have love, I gain nothing. Love is patient, love is kind. It does not envy, it does not boast, it is not proud. It does not dishonor others, it is not self-seeking, it is not easily angered, it keeps no record of wrongs. Love does not delight in evil but rejoices with the truth. It always protects, always trusts, always hopes, and always perseveres.

Love never fails. But where there are prophecies, they will cease; where there are tongues, they will be stilled; where there is knowledge, it will pass away. For we know in part and we prophesy in part, but when completeness comes, what is in part disappears. When I was a child, I talked like a child; I thought like a child, I reasoned like a child. When I became a man, I put the ways of childhood behind me. For now we see only a reflection as in a mirror; then we shall see face to face. Now I know in part; then I shall know fully, even as I am fully known.

And now these three remain: "Faith, Hope and Love. But the Greatest of these is Love."

This perfect love is simple but doesn't come easy and I believe it is a lifelong pursuit. Only God may be able to provide this unconditional love but it's our aim to get as close as humanly possible. I've grown to think of love like a muscle or like working out. I can't go to the gym one day and then instantly, poof, I'm in shape. I have to work on loving and doing loving acts daily and over time love will abide in me. Love can grow and become greater when I practice being more loving.

If we are love and God is love then we are part of God and He is part of us, children from the same one source. When we realize that God is in us and wants what is best for us always then we can live a life full of passion and purpose. Knowing that He has a plan and will always have our best interests in mind. Even when we don't feel like it, He has us exactly where we are supposed to be, He is good and He loves us, no matter what.

CHAPTER 24

INNER PURPOSE

Now take a deep breath. Then take another and awaken to the fact that we have all been given a special gift. I described it early on in my journey as a gift from God but now it's clear to me as a gift of God. Having a presence knowing God in working in your life even when you can't see the reason why is so magical and freeing. No matter where we are at in our lives, God loves us. When we awaken to the belief that it doesn't matter what we've done, no matter how much we have pushed Him away, He is always there and always loves us. As soon as we are ready to make a concious choice we can move forward in our journey knowing we are blessed and do not need to worry about anything. We don't need to save the world; someone has already done that for us!

"I am leaving you with a gift-peace of mind and heart. And the peace I give is a gift the world cannot give. So don't be troubled or afraid." – John 14:27

Now, after our time together my hope is you can start to answer or explore these types of questions:

What do you want to be?

Who are you?

What is your passion and purpose?

Are you willing to go to any lengths to find it?

I will now tell you the answer to how to discover your true self and your purpose and passion.

The answer is <u>You!</u>

It's inside you, it always has been. Now go find it or expand on it. Sometimes we just need a nudge. That's why I want to be an inspirational speaker. It focuses on the "in"-side, being inspired to transform and grow your spirit. Even if I can give just one person a nudge I have accomplished my purpose.

When we learn to control and trust our inner wisdom we can do anything. The ability to tune into those instincts and try to develop them, your skills will grow and make your life full and abundant. It's in the trying that builds momentum and confidence.

The definition of meditation is to become familiar with oneself. Take the time to be still, quiet and listen to your inner self. Its in those moments you will find you have the answers.

When you find and share your inner purpose your outer purpose will shine brighter than ever for the entire world to see. I can't imagine a better life than having the freedom to do the things with the people that I love while providing a good life full of opportunities for my family to grow and live an authetic and purpose filled life.

True freedom comes from within. Freedom is a choice; everyone has feelings of fear, worry, anger and past mistakes that hold them down. The power of finding your purpose and to become aware and control your thinking is you can rise above it.

"Don't copy the behavior and customs of this world, but let God transform you into a new person by changing the way you think. Then you will learn to know God's will for you, which is good and pleasing and perfect." - Romans 12:2

If you're inner purpose matches your outer purpose, and then your life will truly be heaven on earth. If you truly are happy within then you will be living a purpose and passion filled life.

If your mind and soul is right, your world will be right. The beginning of all reform must be in you. It's not what happens to you, it's how you respond. However bad or restricted your circumstances, however bad you think the problem is, you always can turn inward and see some portion of yourself not in order.

Seek and you shall find. Its in the seeking, living with passion, that we find purpose. This saying has been around for thousands of years and is still applicable today and in our everyday lives.

We are just passing through this world, a short stay in the grand scale, so enjoy the miraculous opportunity...and don't forget to pass it on.

The complex magnitude of everything that needed to take place exactly as it did for you to be alive and reading this right now is beyond miraculous.

As you take the journey into finding your purpose and passion, remember, there is not a one size fits all formula. It is your journey. It is a daily, sometimes minutes or hourly, struggle to give in and surrender to that uncomfortable, uneasy, and overwhelming feeling of what we are meant to be. It's not always what we think we want, but what we need in order to be truly fulfilled. When we grab hold of this inner passion we become like a warrior who isn't afraid to die for their cause. There is no perfect recipe for this; with each individual the path is different. The paths are infinite and yours is eternal.

"Trust in the Lord with all your heart, and do not lean on your own understanding. In all your ways acknowledge him, and he will make straight your paths." - Proverbs 3:5-6

It's time for you to start down your path. The moment is upon you to discover what is around that next bend in the river. **The time is NOW, SOMEDAY IS TODAY!**

Start filling up on what works for you to grow, one day at a time. If you do, those days will add up. The more you take action the more you will become aware of whom you were meant to be. You were created for a purpose and it wasn't to be less than what you are capable of.

Once you discover your passion, purpose and unlimited potential, the best part is, you get to experience the magic of giving it all away. You can never give too much away or share too much with others. If you do give it away there will always be more to fill you back up.

The more you give the more you get!

The promises God has for you will come into your life and expand. You will be amazed at what you are capable of, what you discover, who you are and where your passion and purpose can lead you!

There is no perfect blueprint for this journey. Only various guides, suggestions and ways that others have tried from their experiences. Embrace your own personal journey!

So what is your purpose and passion?

Until that someday becomes today when our paths cross, I wish you a very blessed journey. Now go out there and experience life. Look within, unwrap your uniqueness and share your gifts, purpose and passion with others, life's biggest adventure awaits you!

FROM THE AUTHOR

You are a gift to share with the world

As far back as I can remember I felt like my life was designed for greatness and I was destined to fulfill a purposeful and promising life. I didn't know what it was and I didn't know how to harness it but I knew deep down I was instilled with passion and purpose, an inner source, an incessant urge pulling at me. A pull which kept me dreaming and believing anything is possible.

A simple small town barely found on a map and its surrounding countryside was the gracious host to my adventures as a kid. The natural terrain along with some wholesome country cooking, became a great combo to fuel my never ending imagination and exploration throughout my youth. Overall, it was the ideal environment for me to navigate the many nuances life provides. It definitely wasn't perfect but I had a loving childhood filled with a huge extended family, friends, playing multiple sports and experienced mostly good times. When life didn't seem to go my way I either ignored it, ran from it or created my own reality.

My journey to write this started at very young age. I could date it back to first grade when I won a young authors competition for the book I wrote, "The Bear that went to Space". I've always felt a connection to my inner soul when writing and I was quite the storyteller. Sometimes it seemed like I used my imagination to entertain myself or my peers and other times it worked well to get out of trouble.

I performed very well in most subjects and had a fairly easy time getting good grades and finishing my assignments with minimal effort. English was, at times, the subject which challenged me the most, which I find ironic because here I am writing a book. My mind nat-

urally and somewhat easily connected with numbers and equations and systems in math and science, even social studies, but what drove my soul to new heights is when I was encouraged to write poems and short stories by my fourth grade teacher. My thoughts and imagination filled my world with powerful emotions and time stood still as the words and what they meant to me flowed onto those pages. It wasn't like math where there only was one answer. There were infinite ways the story could play out and I felt timeless, eternal and truly alive coming up with those rhythmic lyrics and whimsical tales.

My writings and stories were well received. I even won a competition for public speaking on the subject of wolf conversation in fourth grade. Being selected the winner felt great, but that didn't matter to me. What I enjoyed was how fulfilled I felt and how activated my inner spirit was when I wrote and spoke from the heart.

It didn't seem like it at the time but grade school went by quickly. It's like waiting for your birthday when you're eight, the days feel like eternity, the anticipation is agonizing, but in reality each day covers the same amount of time. Middle school was a blur and then came high school. As the years went by my imagination and insatiable quest for more was always burning within. I dabbled in poetry and continued writing, but packing as much fun as possible in life, playing sports and socializing with friends became my priorities. As each year in high school progressed so did my will, coupled with a growing ego, disguised as ambition, rocketed me forward into a new realm of confidence. I never sat still long enough with my feelings for them to catch up with me.

My senior year of high school I felt like I had arrived. I was the homecoming king, excelled in sports and was voted class president. Every day I went to high school my confidence rose. After graduation, what on all accounts could be considered "The epic summer of fun". I arrived at college ready to play football and take on the world.

College was a logical and enticing choice. It was so full of spirit, freedom and endless possibilities. After two semesters of rotating between going to class, playing sports and partying on the weekends, summer came and I decided to join the army to serve my country through the universities ROTC program.

I somehow came to the conclusion it was a better option than waking up each morning at 4 am and heading off to the factory where I worked the summer prior. This is where irony sets in. Instead that summer I attended basic training, woke up at 4 am, and got my butt kicked for 10 weeks.

I will admit it did give me a new perspective that I could get through anything. When I returned my sophomore year of college and reported for football practice I was a lean, mean, fighting machine. I was physically in the best shape of my life. But I don't know deep down if I had the true heart for field combat, on the football field or the battlefield. However, I did make the team and even though I didn't get much playing time, I enjoyed staying active, the comradery and it kept me connected socially and always in the loop for the best parties.

College is freedom and it is what you make it. I enjoyed learning, the social gatherings and learning new worldly concepts. I also enjoyed staying active and feeling healthy was always an important part of my life. With freedom there is also responsibility. I missed that lesson on a hot August day.

Shortly after I turned 21 years old I celebrated by getting a new motorcycle, what happened next shifted my world. Within hours of picking up that steel horse, I lay face down on the asphalt, broken and tattered; the accident was a deafening blow. I was carted into emergency surgery within minutes of getting to the hospital. After nine screws, a metal plate, two surgeries and a permanent titanium rod in my tibia later I somehow believed this must have happened for a reason.

Although I wouldn't understand why this had to happen until many years later, I made the most of my nine months on crutches. I figured I might as well focus on my studies and trudged my way to finishing college with a degree. I moved forward with as much vigor as possible and stayed as active as I could muster each day. I have to admit; I developed some great skills and got quite nimble on two crutches and only one leg. I also got pretty darn good at driving with my left foot while my right leg was propped comfortably across the front seat of my 92' Olds Cutlass. I made a name for myself on campus riding a bicycle with a pair of crutches strapped across the back. I even started a bike club called the Night Hawks, which was essentially a posy or gang of four or five passionate college folks riding bicycles around at night ready for whatever the dark would bring.

Thinking I was a hopeless romantic and utilizing some self-pity, I think I might have used my broken leg to my advantage and got a few people to feel sorry for me and help me along the way.

One day the energy of the universe aligned just right and my life changed unexpectedly from thinking like a hopeless romantic to becoming one.

I was supposed to be sitting in class learning how to coordinate special events but it was the sweet yet confident voice which spoke up which grabbed my undivided attention that day instead. As I lifted my head from my elaborate doodle I had so majestically been drawing, it was like seeing an angel for the first time. She was an angel wearing shapely gray slacks, a very nice form-fitting purple blouse, and gorgeous hair and dark brown sensual eyes that had the perfect balance of sweet innocence and seduction. And her smile, wow, it was one of those smiles which made the world a happier place to live in. Now, you would have thought that I had seen her before since she was in the same major in college and it was half way through the semester. Like any unexpected life changing moment, my eyes opened, I saw and felt something that I still can't quite explain. I guess you could say I suddenly had a flash of genius, as I gazed across the classroom, it was like a grappling claw or X-ray seduction beam drew me to this woman and she enveloped me with a spell that instantly changed my mindset.

I thought I had fallen in love before and been heartbroken. I didn't want to feel the pain of heartbreak again. When I take time to reflect on the gut churning and emotionally imploding feeling of heartbreak, I believe I could look back to first grade once again, when I gave the cutest girl in first grade a ring I found on the playground next to the merry-go-round during recess in return for her love. Her mom apparently didn't think that her daughter should be courted so young and made her return the ring the next day thus ending our twelve hour courtship and my heart was broken for the first time. First grade imprinted my mind and heart with a lot of life's grand lessons.

It's crazy how heartbreak in first grade and heartbreak when you're a freshman or sophomore in college can give you the same gut wrenching madness, and due to this, I had told myself I was going to stay single, finish up college and go see the world. After getting dealt a heartbreak freshman and sophomore years of college, I didn't want anything to do with that type of blow for a long time, if ever.

But as I sat there in RECREATION 300 class, trying not to be obvious as I glanced at her thinking maybe I was still sleeping. Maybe it was a vivid day dream. But I felt like that child in first grade again, it was if time stood still for a few moments. She ignited that same inner pull and spirit I had felt as a child towards something bigger than myself and I felt propelled to try again. The past didn't matter in that moment.

After class that day, I took a leap of faith, and asked her if she needed help with our class project. I hadn't been too interested in the project prior to that, but suddenly I was overly motivated to offer my assistance. My priority in that moment was to give her my undivided attention. It didn't matter what classes or obligations I had the rest of the day.

From her perspective, it was probably as weird as it was in first grade when a boy comes up to a girl and offers to give you a ring he found on the playground for your love, but I was a tad less obvious then that, I think. At the very least I was hoping she would leave class that day a little intrigued. I couldn't fight or resist how I felt and the clarity I had in that moment. I guess if I was dreaming then I had nothing to lose. I knew there was a chance I might get hurt again but the feeling of wanting to get to know her was worth the risk. I approached this relationship differently. I was living in the moment. I was given a gift of new found awareness... It's like a spirit filled and guided me. I *balanced patience with a steady confidence that persisted and allowed me to become vulnerable yet assured. I forced myself to believe and have faith that the type of love I always imagined was possible.*

I fell in love with that wonderfully beautiful woman that I now get to wake up to each and every day. My wife is someone who challenges me to continue to be better and discover new ways to view everyday life as a blessing. I could go on and on about the mystery of why and how we fell in love and how we continue to grow together, but only God knows, and that might be for another book.

College was over, and it was time for the "real world". A phrase I wasn't fond of until recent years. The stars continued to align and we were fortunate to land full-time employment in the same city.

My marriage proposal took place on an ordinary night. I hid the ring as I was waiting for the perfect moment. But is there such thing as "The perfect moment"? I'm not sure, but I know there are ideal moments to take advantage of and make a choice that will forever change your life. That moment came, as I stood in my kitchen mixing up some macaroni and cheese in the kitchen.

I got out my guitar and sang a poem I wrote about how it was simple but I knew it wouldn't be easy (plus it rhymed with macaroni and cheesy) but the journey was going to be so worth it. I got down on one knee, and just like that my best friend said yes and we were engaged. I guess I just couldn't wait any longer. It was in the moment and it was real, not all drawn out, preplanned and made up to be something superficially glamorous, which makes it simply unforgettable.

Within a year we were married and approximately ten months after our honeymoon, our first son was born.

The years went by, hard work and a positive attitude led to promotions at work and within a few years our quaint house got upgraded to a bigger house which we filled with more kids.

They say life happens in the blink of an eye and that is how those first six year felt. Flash forward six years and four kids later. After years of fighting my way through my own ambitions and expectations, I awoke to the reality that I wasn't the man I wanted to be and I didn't feel fulfilled. I had fought a lot to stay a step ahead of those feelings but had lost touch with who I was and felt a void in my soul. I realized I had dedicated my efforts to many things but never remained fully committed to the quest of discovering my true purpose. I wasn't following God's plan for me I was trying to follow my own. I had lost touch with God. I blamed it on outside circumstances and other people, but it was truly my own fault, and in that moment, what seemed like the picturesque white-picket- fence lifestyle, from the outside looking in, stood a confused soul.

For years I had kept busy and didn't allow myself to address my feelings, faults and negative actions. I thought if I ignored or denied them enough, telling myself they weren't real, I guess I was hoping eventually they would just magically disappear. I was scared of what I might find. Through the emotional ups and downs and my delusional perception of the real world. It finally caught up to me, and it was time to do something about it.

Back in college I had started journaling off and on saying someday I was going to write a book. I would say someday I'm going to do this or become that, but never did it. It ultimately took a seed of despair to sprout to start writing this. I hit a point where I surrendered to the fact that I had a choice. I was forced once again to make a big decision and took a leap of faith. This time into a journey to find myself.

I started a quest to find out who I really was and rediscover my purpose. I could have continued living out a pretty good life, but I knew deep down that I would wake up one day with regret. Life has a way of pushing our dreams down. I couldn't bury them with any more pain or struggles. I didn't want to look back and think about where my big dreams had come and gone. I decided I needed to accept that I wasn't the man I wanted to be. I didn't know what that meant but I was going to, no, I HAD TO, find out.

This started a journey almost five years ago of letting go of the parts of me that didn't make me the best version of myself. I began working towards developing myself into the person that I was put on this earth to be. I felt there were some parts of my life I needed to fix for other's sake, but this had to be something that I needed to do for myself.

I'm definitely not proclaiming to be an expert, have all the answers or introduce you to new earth shattering ideas. I'm just a normal person just like you trying to find purpose in this journey called life. I believe the answers to our passion, purpose and true path are within us. The processes that guide us have been around for thousands of years. It's literately quite simple, just not always easy.

This was a process for me. I don't know what is going to work for you to discover or enlarge your passion and purpose, but, I do know some of these simple practices will help you succeed in finding your destiny.

I have heard that authors write what they need at the time to push them through to new heights and maybe that is what has taken place with this book. My hope is we can take this journey together. Let's go into that uncomfortable place and dig deep to discover and practice new ways to expand our passion, purpose and better ourselves along the way. I trust you will find some of the thoughts, ideas and methods that have worked thus far for me to be worth trying out. If not, at the very least, if it propels you to search for what works for you or what you've been unwilling to attempt in the past, then I feel I may have helped. I'm hoping some of the messages in this book will inspire you to discover the gifts within you. I'm even more hopeful you will realize you are a unique and special gift and life's greatest adventure is sharing yourself with the world. As you enthusiastically engage in pursuing your dreams, passion and purpose the journey may be tough but the rewards are bountiful.

What started as a spark ignited a fire within me and the flame grew and quickly enveloped my soul. It continued churning and stirring through my mind and soul into a wildfire. It was a desire that had been restlessly waiting for me to take action. It waited patiently until the time was right. The moment had come once again to make a change and take action and I pushed forward with no expectations other than to become my true self and help others.

What started out as a working document with bullet points for an endnote presentation for a national conference became a platform to my dream of writing this book. During the past five years I became committed to this dream, ok, maybe at times a little obsessed. I worked on myself daily, started taking action, speaking at various conferences, workshops, working a full time job, raising 5 kids, being Cub Scout leader, coach, husband, accomplishing much and failing often all while learning to better myself and build my character.

I truly hope this book inspires at least one person and sparks their own journey. I believe that if you truly pursue your passion and purpose, you can accomplish anything!

When I was putting my first endnote presentation together I focused my message and theme in the hope of inspiring others to find their passion and purpose. I began jotting down ideas and reflected on some of the various practices or themes that worked for me. I wrote down bullet points which helped me practice shaping new habits which enlarged my purpose, bettered my life and added joy to my journey. The themes of the categories included Passion, Purpose, Presence, Perspective, Progress, and Prayer and my mind just started accumulating words that started with the letter P. This is why you will find so many chapter headlines starting with the letter P in this book. Once I focus on something and it gets drawn into my mind, it multiplies and becomes my reality. This time my reality became the quest of how words starting with the letter P could help to organize my thoughts.

I also developed a daily practice of journaling and stuck with it. I "pressed on" journaling each and every day for an entire year and guided the creation of most of the pages you will find within this book. One of the entries I wrote, that inspired me to continue, I would love to share with you.

"Press on! For it is a sure thing. As predictable as the seasons and as cool and promising as the early morning dew. From which the seeds soak in moisture to nourish and breathe life into sprouts of warmth,

joy and love. Sometimes droughts come but don't lose your faith. Surely press on! Be steadfast and do not waver. For in your love, as in God's love, it never waivers. Even in the darkest forest, deepest cave or dryest desert. Stand in the sunshine of the solution as focusing on the darkness brings despair, sickness and death. Now, press on, knowing you will be rewarded with the grace and love which has already been granted."

I wish to thank all the people that were involved in writing this. It seems almost impossible to reach everyone, as I believe I am made up of a small piece of everyone I have ever met in my life, and many more I haven't. There are some people that contributed larger than others and they probably have a little bigger piece making up my puzzle. But if I have ever met you, even in a random moment, or through the divine connection that brought my life, its experiences and messages to me, you are more than likely in some way, form or fashion, part of me and thus part of this book.

This is the first time in my life where I've allowed myself to be truly loved and chosen to love others by being my true self. This journey didn't come without some ups and downs and there were times where I thought I wasn't cut out. At times we all want to settle for life just being good enough.

I was blessed to have this passionate urge instilled in me from my creator, an inner universal presence and power, which I call God. I was reluctant to listen but He waited patiently, helped steer my direction and stuck with me.

Once I started the journey, I was hooked and I knew I needed to keep pressing forward, sharing my passion and carrying a message became the sole part of my purpose. Your passion is for you, your purpose is how your passion can help others. Our purpose is much bigger than any one of us. Living your life with passion, purpose and helping others discover their passion and purpose can truly change the world.

We never know when this spark will happen, where it will take place or when experiences, people or moments are going to come into our

157

lives, urging and inspiring us to take action. Its God's timing not ours. It's not when we want it to happen but when we need it to happen. We all have a deeply profound purpose and maybe it's time you find or reignite yours.

From the deepest parts of my soul, I felt like if I didn't write this book, I wasn't giving justice or respect to God, myself and to all those that have helped and continue to support and love me. Thank you and please enjoy the journey.

Made in the USA
Coppell, TX
17 January 2020

14617725R00092